D1558888

BREAKING THE STEM STEREOTYPE

BREAKING THE STEM STEREOTYPE

Reaching Girls in Early Childhood

Amanda Alzena Sullivan

ROWMAN & LITTLEFIELD
Lanham • Boulder • New York • London

Published by Rowman & Littlefield
An imprint of The Rowman & Littlefield Publishing Group, Inc.
4501 Forbes Boulevard, Suite 200, Lanham, Maryland 20706
www.rowman.com

6 Tinworth Street, London SE11 5AL

British Library Cataloguing in Publication Information Available

Library of Congress Cataloging-in-Publication Data

Names: Sullivan, Amanda (Amanda Alzena) author.
Title: Breaking the STEM stereotype : reaching girls in early childhood / Amanda Alzena Sullivan.
Description: Lanham, Maryland : Rowman & Littlefield, 2019. | Includes bibliographical references. | Summary: "Breaking the STEM Stereotype delves into the reasons behind the persistent gender disparity between men and women in STEM fields. It explores the powerful role of stereotypes and provides parents and educators with tips and resources on how to begin dispelling stereotypes and engaging girls with STEM during the foundational early childhood years"—Provided by publisher.
Identifiers: LCCN 2019012308 (print) | LCCN 2019981213 (ebook) | ISBN 9781475842043 (cloth) | ISBN 9781475842050 (ebook)
Subjects: LCSH: Science—Study and teaching (Early childhood)—United States. | Mathematics—Study and teaching (Early childhood)—United States. | Girls—Education (Early childhood)—United States. | Sex differences in education.
Classification: LCC LB1139.5.S35 S87 2019 (print) | LCC LB1139.5.S35 (ebook) | DDC 372.35/044—dc23
LC record available at https://lccn.loc.gov/2019012308
LC ebook record available at https://lccn.loc.gov/2019981213

CONTENTS

FOREWORD

Why do we find fewer women than men in technology-related professions? Why do girls think of themselves as "not good" at math and science? What are the differences in teaching approaches, if any, needed to capture the imagination of both boys and girls in scientific and technological domains of learning? What are the realities and myths surrounding gender stereotypes? At what age should we start educational programs to address these stereotypes? These are some of the questions that Amanda Sullivan seeks to explore in this book. Writing about gender and STEM (Science, Technology, Engineering, and Mathematics education) is trendy nowadays. However, Amanda became fascinated with this topic long ago, not only due to her intellectual curiosity, but also through personal experience.

I met Amanda in the fall of 2010, when she was just starting her master's degree program at the Eliot-Pearson Department of Child Study and Human Development. She approached me because she wanted to be involved in my DevTech Research Group. At DevTech, we aim to understand how new technologies that engage in coding, robotics, and making can play a positive role in children's development and learning.

Our research covers three dimensions: theoretical contributions, design of new technologies, and empirical work to test and evaluate the theory and the technologies. We create programming languages such as KIBO robotics (https://sites.tufts.edu/devtech/research/kibo-robot/) and ScratchJr (https://sites.tufts.edu/devtech/research/scratchjr/), as well as teaching materials and pedagogical strategies for the professional development of early childhood educators and for community engagement.

Our longtime commitment is to inspire sustainable and scalable evidence-based programs for young children that promote the learning of programming and computational thinking with a playful, developmentally appropriate approach. We understand coding as a literacy of the 21st century, one that provides tools for self-expression and problem solving, collaboration, and community building.

Amanda had a background in drama and loved to work with children, but had no previous experience with technology of any kind. She wanted to help girls grow up confident, learning about all the things she never had the chance to explore. During our first meeting, she was apologetic. What she did not realize is that these characteristics made her most appealing to me. At DevTech, I like to have a mixed group of people who can think creatively and work hard, but who are strong at communicating with others because they truly care about something. Amanda exemplified all of this. She truly cared about girls and technology.

From the beginning, Amanda designed curricular experiences for KIBO robots that would attract both boys and girls. As Amanda started to gain her own sense of confidence and competence with technology, she was able to overcome stereotypes she herself had fallen into, and she became one of the pillars of my research group, completing her MA, her PhD, and her postdoctoral work.

Like most child development experts, Amanda believed that the issue of women's underrepresentation in STEM starts long before women enter the career world, and understood that early experiences are critical to success later in life. Therefore, for her doctoral thesis, she explored gender issues by designing and implementing a study in several early childhood classrooms using KIBO. This book grows out of what she learned doing her doctoral work and her passion. However, this book is more than that.

In addition to presenting current research on gender inequity of women in STEM, this book provides insights and strategies to reach girls beginning in early childhood to address this inequity. By reading this book, parents, teachers, and any adult who is in contact with children will be empowered to bring about change, not just for girls and women, but for everyone living, learning, and working together.

Marina Umaschi Bers, PhD
Professor and Chair, Eliot-Pearson Department of
Child Study and Human Development
Adjunct Professor, Computer Science Department
Tufts University
Author of *Coding as a Playground: Programming and
Computational Thinking in the Early Childhood Classroom* (2017)

ACKNOWLEDGMENTS

First and foremost, I must thank my loving and supportive family. To my husband Adam, thank you for your unwavering support of all my endeavors. You believed that my research and ideas on this topic could be a book long before there was an offer to write and publish it. I'm grateful not only for your emotional support, but for your dedicated editing, your thoughtful critiques, your advice during long car rides and dinners, and for keeping me calm during moments of writer's block and panic.

To my son Sidney, I wrote this book during the first year you came into my life: and what a joyous and momentous year it was! You are my muse in so many ways. Each day you remind me about the value of playful learning, of exploring our curiosities, and of seeing the world with awe and wonder. Thank you for inspiring and motivating your mom!

To my brother Sean, the real writer in the family, thank you for your love and support. I write about the value of role-modeling in this book. I don't think I would have accomplished anything in my life without the examples that you set, and I am forever grateful.

To my parents, thank you for always supporting me and believing in my dreams, even when life circumstances were difficult. Thank you for instilling in me the belief that education is important and hard work pays off. I strive to pass these beliefs and values on to all the children I work and care for.

I also must thank all of my colleagues, mentors, and friends at Tufts, especially at the DevTech Research Group. I wholeheartedly wish to thank my mentor, Professor Marina Umaschi Bers. Marina, you have been my ultimate female role model in STEM, in academia, and in life. Thank you for believing in my research, for supporting me, and for allowing me to pursue this topic with you. This book is inspired by the work I did for my dissertation under your guidance. I am humbled to have been your student, and forever grateful you took a chance on me.

To all my colleagues at DevTech over the years, thank you for your support, your advice, and for stimulating conversations about gender, education, technology, and STEM. In particular, many thanks to Emily Relkin for your thoughtful advice and edits during my early writing process for this book. You are brilliant, and I was so lucky that you selflessly volunteered your time and input. I can't wait to pay it forward when you write your own book!

To my friends, too many to list, thank you for your support and love over the years. Amanda Strawhacker, thank you for your friendship and advice throughout this process. I am so grateful for every article you sent my way, every motivating Gchat, and every milestone you celebrated with me. I don't think I could ever write anything without our secret writing rewards Google doc!

To my friend Safiya, who also happens to be the most talented writer I know, thank you for your love and support in everything I do, including venturing into the world of books for the first time. Thank you for sharing in all my struggles and successes in over a decade of friendship. I owe so much to you.

To my friend Katie (and all my other mom friends), thank you for sharing in all the joys and struggles of new motherhood with me. Your ideas and approaches to parenting have helped inspire so much of this book. But moreover, I simply could not have gotten through this past year as a new parent without your support!

Thank you to my editor Sarah for reaching out to me and making all of this possible to begin with. Your insightful edits and critiques along with your enthusiastic support for my work has made this such a rewarding experience for me.

Finally, thank you to all of my teachers growing up, and all the amazing professors and mentors I had along my academic journey at Bennington College and Tufts University. I am especially grateful to everyone in the Department of Child Study and Human Development at Tufts. I truly believe that good teachers can change lives. So many of you have changed mine.

INTRODUCTION

Female Underrepresentation in Science, Technology, Engineering, and Mathematics (STEM)—And What We Can Do About It

How are you reading this book? Are you reading it on an iPad or e-reader? Did you use your computer to buy this book on Amazon or another website? Now close your eyes and imagine the person who designed and built your iPad or computer. Imagine the person who maintains and updates the website on which you purchased this book. What do they look like? What are their behavioral characteristics? Don't censor yourself or your thoughts. What are your honest first reactions?

If you are like many other people, when you think of technical careers, you picture a man. When you think of human-engineered products in general, you may also think of a man. Just think of how commonly the word "*man*-made" is used compared to human-made or human-engineered. Maybe when you think about websites and computers, you also picture a "nerd" or an introvert. You may envision someone sitting alone at a desk, hunched over a computer, writing lines of code in solitude. Perhaps you picture someone socially awkward or antisocial who prefers working with technology over the company of coworkers. These are just a few common stereotypes people hold about engineers, programmers, and other people working in technical fields.

When it comes to STEM (Science, Technology, Engineering, and Mathematics), rampant stereotypes pervade these fields. Many of these happen to be gender stereotypes. Almost every woman at some point in her life has heard that "girls aren't good at math." Whether we *believe* these stereotypes or not, the truth of the matter is they have an impact. Today, women still are not well represented in many STEM fields.

Over the past half century, women have made incredible progress in many traditionally male-dominated professions such as law, business, and the military. But in many STEM fields, progress is being made at a far slower rate. In the United States, men continue to outnumber women in numerous STEM careers, particularly in technical fields such as computer science and engineering (National Science Foundation, 2017). The representation of women in science and engineering is substantially lower than their representation in the U.S. population. According to a National Science Foundation special report (2017), the fields of computer science, physics, and engineering are still overwhelmingly male. In the decade before this report was published, both the number and proportion of computer sciences bachelor's degrees earned by women actually *declined*.

WHERE ARE ALL THE WOMEN?

The statistics of women in STEM are as disturbing as they are puzzling. They have prompted me to ask the question: where are all the women? Decades of research has shown there is not one easy answer. Researchers have uncovered dozens of factors working *against* women and girls when it comes to STEM—factors that have been identified by scholars across a wide range of fields.

Psychologists have studied the impact of implicit attitudes and stereotypes; feminist theorists have examined the role of masculine influences embedded in our culture; advertising experts have looked at the role of gender in marketing of STEM products; media experts have examined how boys and girls are portrayed in popular culture; and educators have looked at curriculum content and social dynamics in school. All of these factors taken together—along with recent accounts of sexual harassment in tech fields, workplace discrimination, and pay inequity—have contributed to a society that simply does not support women who pursue STEM careers the same way it supports men.

This is a problem. This is not just a problem for women; it is a problem for businesses and creative innovation in our society in general. In the next decade, it is estimated that the United States will need 1.7 million more engineers and computing professionals, and the perspectives and the talent of women—who make up half the population—must not be ignored (Corbett & Hill, 2015). According to research by McKinsey & Company, which examined proprietary data sets for 366 public companies across a range of industries in the United States, Canada, Latin America, and the United Kingdom, gender and ethnic diversity is linked with increased profits for companies (Hunt, Layton, & Prince, 2015; Hunt, Prince, Dixon-Fyle, & Yee, 2017). Companies in the top quartile for gender diversity were 15% more likely to have financial returns above their respective national industry medians (Hunt et al., 2015). Additionally, the researchers also found a relationship between racial and ethnic diversity and improved financial performance in the United States (Hunt et al., 2015).

Underrepresentation of women is not only bad for business, but also leads to an ethical problem. When women are severely underrepresented in STEM industries, many technical innovations are made based solely on the opinions, judgments, and physicality of men (Williams, 2014). The end result? Smartphones that don't fit women's hands as well as men's (Tufekci, 2013; Ryan, 2013). Health apps that ignore women's menstrual cycles (Duhaime-Ross, 2014). Virtual assistants that have more difficulty answering women's questions than men's questions, and can suggest help for a heart attack, but cannot answer questions about rape or domestic abuse (Chemaly, 2016; Miner et al., 2016). Diversity of genders, races, ethnicities, and experiences in the STEM workforce is sorely needed, not only to promote creativity and innovation, but to ensure that a range of views representative of our diverse population are considered in the design of products and tools we all rely on every day.

I am not alone in seeking to address this problem. Since 2010, it has been thrilling to see a growing crop of tools, programs, and interventions that have emerged with the goal of supporting women in STEM. Many of these amazing programs, such as Scientista, Girls Who Code, and the Women in Engineering Proactive Network (WEPAN), focus on supporting young women during the peak "career decision" years: during adolescence and in college. Despite these programs, the gender divide in STEM persists.

These programs for adolescent and college-aged women can have a powerful impact, but I wonder, why are we waiting so long to reach young women? In many cases, these programs and interventions happen *after* young women have already decided they do not have a strong interest in STEM.

We have seen that during adolescence, the gender gap between boys and girls in standardized STEM test scores and STEM course-taking becomes more defined. By high school, male students are more likely than female students to take the standardized exams closely associated with the fields of engineering and computing (Corbett & Hill, 2015). Females in high school are also less likely to decide to take Advanced Placement (AP) level computer science classes, or express interest in pursuing an undergraduate computer science major than males (Doerschuk, Liu, & Mann, 2007; Gal-Ezer & Stephenson, 2009).

Clearly, for many girls, middle school and high school interventions come too late. Because of this, programs and interventions that take place during adolescence are attempting to *fix* a gender gap problem rather than *prevent* a problem to begin with. So why not reach girls while they are in their foundational early childhood years and throughout elementary school? Why not reach them when they are beginning to choose clubs and select hobbies that will guide their academic experience for many years to come? Then, continue to support them throughout their adolescence, college, and in their careers?

As an educator and child development researcher, I believe the issue of women's underrepresentation in STEM starts long before women enter the career world. Like most child development specialists, I believe that early experiences are critical to success later in life. We need to expose girls to quality STEM content as they are growing up and exploring their identities and interests; while they are still gaining confidence in their abilities and still deciding what they are "good at" and what they enjoy. By reaching *all* children beginning in early childhood, we will provide them with equal opportunities to pursue the hobbies, passions, and careers they are interested in further down the line.

> xix

THE POWER OF EARLY EXPERIENCES

Early experiences, conversations, and memories matter. To this day, I still remember people saying things like "your brother is better at math because he is a boy" when I was growing up. Maybe it was said as a joke, maybe it was said as a passing comment, but nonetheless, it is a statement I remember.

I remember anxiety and sweaty palms as I struggled with timed math tests beginning in elementary school; an anxiety that I never shook or outgrew. I had this performance anxiety despite actually *enjoying* my math classes. I remember being supported and encouraged by teachers to pursue drama, writing, and art, but can't for the life of me remember being invited to join a robotics or chemistry club at school. I did not learn about any female engineers or scientists growing up, nor did I meet any women working in these fields. These early experiences gradually became more powerful than my initial enjoyment and excitement for math and science as a young child.

In addition to the explicit comments and experiences, I remember math and science having an *implicit* air of masculinity. Part of this may have been my role models. My older brother really *was* good at math, and I admired what seemed to be his "natural" ability in this domain. When it came time for help with math or science homework, my mom felt she could not help me and so I looked to my brother or father for guidance. Like my brother, my father also seemed to have a "natural" inclination toward mathematics. I began to see math performance as an innate ability (something you are either naturally good at or not), and not a learned skill that I could practice and get better at.

Meanwhile, my mother was always there to role-model socializing and people skills. She fluctuated between full-time motherhood and working in hospitality. She was (and still is) very much a "people person" who excels at socializing and putting people at ease. She did not attend college, nor did any other women in her family. Instead, she drew on her natural ability to joke, tell stories, and befriend almost anyone. I admired these skills in her, and these skills became associated as feminine traits in my mind.

Like most parents, my mother and father believed my brother and I could be anything we wanted when we grew up—and they told us as much! And I have no doubt that if I had said I wanted to be an astronaut or mathematician when I grew up, they would have supported me. But with no *explicit* teachings, the role-modeling I received at home subtly taught me: math and science = male, while communication and interpersonal skills = female.

I later found out how common this was when I discovered that many of my female friends had very similar experiences growing up. The role-modeling I received at home was mirrored by the modeling of teachers and mentors I met in school, as well as my childhood experiences with friends and the messages I received through the media. I remember the "star students" in my math classes being boys and my female friends complaining about how much they hated math or that they weren't "math people."

What I did not know at the time was that these early comments, experiences, and *lack* of certain experiences were shaping my path in many unseen ways. Beginning in early childhood and throughout middle and high school, girls and young women are exposed to stereotypes that inform ideas about their identity, abilities, and interest in STEM fields. By age five, children are already demonstrating gender-stereotyped knowledge about being male or female. Young children are not immune to the gender stereotypes that govern our culture. They are just beginning to take in these stereotypes and ingrain them, perhaps shifting their life paths in unseen directions.

WHY THIS BOOK?

I have been battling stereotypes my whole life. Growing up poor, each day at school I faced stereotypes about my intelligence, capability, and social skills based on my appearance, clothes, or where I lived. Being biracial (Southeast Asian and Caucasian), I have faced countless stereotypes based on how people perceived my so-called "ambiguous" ethnic background. And being female, I have battled gender stereotypes about my professional aspirations, my role as a wife and mother, my physical appearance, as well as my capability in STEM fields.

Like many women, I have faced harassment, demeaning statements, and discouragement. Looking back, the most painful thing is that somewhere along the way, I *believed* these stereotypes. It took amazing female role models, a supportive academic community, and learning about the impact of stereotypes during my college and graduate school years to begin shifting my mindset and gaining confidence in my skills.

This book is sparked by my own experiences as a child and by my experiences with children as an educator. Teaching STEM classes, I have met countless young girls struggling with the same stereotypes that I grew up facing. I have met so many well-meaning parents and educators who don't know what they should be saying or doing to ensure girls have equal opportunities in STEM. Based on these experiences, I was inspired to advocate for girls in STEM. I want children today to have the tools, experiences, and opportunities that I did not have growing up. I believe children should have access to high-quality STEM programs regardless of race, gender, and socioeconomic status.

As a STEM educator for young children, I strive to create fun, playful, and social opportunities for young children to explore STEM that is process (rather than *product*) oriented and celebrates making mistakes. I integrate my love of drama, the arts, and music with STEM in order to reach a wider range of children. As a researcher, I strive to evaluate tools and curricula in order to determine the best ways to reach girls with STEM content, increasing their interest and confidence in these fields. My goal is not to make every child grow up to be a mathematician or an engineer. My goal is to make sure every child has an equal opportunity to pursue these fields if and when they want to.

During my training in child development, I studied with Professor Marina Umaschi Bers, the director of the Developmental Technologies (DevTech) Research Group at Tufts University and the current chair of the Department of Child Study and Human Development. Working with Marina and DevTech as a doctoral student (and later a postdoctoral researcher), I spent over eight years exploring the power of early childhood STEM interventions and the positive impact they can have on all young children, regardless of gender. I originally joined the group hoping to teach and do research (which I did). But I was also gaining valuable mathematical and technical skills, and began to counteract the stereotypes I once believed about myself and my abilities. Not only did I master advanced statistics and math concepts in my research and coursework, at DevTech I also learned that I could code, I could solder, I could assemble robots—who knew?!

My growing confidence in my own STEM abilities prompted me to begin designing coding and robotics initiatives specifically to engage young girls (kindergarten through second grade) in technology and engineering and address the masculine stereotypes they were forming about these fields. In my doctoral research at Tufts, I found that when using developmentally appropriate materials and curricula, coding and robotics can significantly increase girls' level of interest in being an engineer when they grow up. I discovered that early childhood initiatives with robotics also increases the percentage of children (both boys and girls) who view robotics as gender-neutral rather than "for boys" or "for girls."

My research also confirmed some of the things I anecdotally knew from my years as an educator: young children are confronted with and are incorporating a whole host of gender stereotypes about the technologies and human-engineered products they encounter every day. Their ideas about games, apps, technologies, and toys are developing at the same time as their sense of gender and their understanding of gender roles.

I interviewed dozens of young children and heard things like "girls don't like building things that are harder like LEGOs" and learned that children generally considered more STEM-based digital games "for boys" rather than "for girls" or for all children. I also learned about the power of seemingly mundane experiences with parents, teachers, and caregivers. For example, in one interview, a young boy explained that his experiences with the way his mom and dad each approach using LEGOs influenced his belief that boys are better at building:

Interviewer: Can girls build as well as boys?

Child: No, because boys are excellent at building because my dad can build, like, any LEGO set. Whenever he gives me a LEGO set, he builds them, any of them. Like, I don't know how he did this, but he told me he didn't build LEGOs when he was a kid, so he just knows.

Interviewer: Really? And he does it now? He builds LEGOs now? [Pause] What about your mom?

Child: I don't . . . no, she's not good.

Interviewer: She's not good at LEGOs?

Child: She always looks at the directions and she doesn't know which piece goes on [each] piece.

Whether we know it or not, everything we say to young children, and how we behave around them, matters. And most of the time our actions speak louder than words. If a child sees his or her father approach LEGO building with such gusto that he literally builds them *for* (rather than *with*) the child, this sends a message. If the child's mother approaches building so hesitantly that she focuses only on following directions rather than having fun and improvising, this also sends a message. If children only see their fathers build IKEA furniture or only see their mothers pack lunches, this sends a message.

As a parent myself, I understand personally what a heavy weight this is! We cannot be perfect. But we *can* make small changes in the way we work with young children to set them up for success when it comes to STEM. My interviews led me to believe that young children ages four through eight are at the perfect age to begin counteracting these stereotypes through the programs we implement in schools, the way parents and teachers role-model for children, and the types of products and materials that are available to help boys and girls to learn about STEM.

My goal for this book is to reach beyond those in academic circles who read dissertations, research articles, and data published in peer-reviewed journals. My goal for this book is to reach *you*: the people who actually have the power to make a difference in the lives of children. This means educators, camp counselors, parents, grandparents, aunts and uncles, and other caregivers. It also means the designers of technologies, the creators of clubs and curricula, librarians, computer lab coordinators, and all those who work with young children every day.

This book is set up in three parts. Part I presents the current state of the gender divide in STEM, looking at each component: science, technology, engineering, and mathematics. As we'll see, not all STEM fields are created equally. In some areas of STEM, particularly in the natural and social sciences, we see a strong representation by women. We'll explore why, then, in mathematics and the technical STEM fields such a drastic gender disparity continues to persist.

The second part looks at young children's developing sense of gender and gender identity. It explores how and why stereotypes are developed and ingrained during this gender development process. We will look at the phenomenon of "stereotype threat," or anxiety over the perception that one's performance will be seen through the lens of a negative stereotype, and how this impacts girls and women in STEM (Spencer, Steele, & Quinn, 1999; Steele, 1997). We will explore the perpetuation of stereotypes in the media and advertising, as well as the impact of role-modeling on the development of these stereotypes.

The final part of this book will empower you to enact change. It will describe the types of books, tools, activities, and curricula that can be used to begin introducing STEM to young girls in a fun, playful, and developmentally appropriate way, both within and outside of the school setting. We will consider the pros and cons of gender-neutral products and programs, as well as tools and programs specifically designed and marketed toward girls. Perhaps most importantly, we will consider the impact of what we say and do around young children. We will consider making small but powerful changes in our own actions in order to foster as unbiased and supportive a community of learners as possible.

WHAT ABOUT YOUNG BOYS?

If you are a parent or educator, you might be wondering how young boys fit into this equation. I am a mother to a young boy myself, and I can tell you that I have grappled with this issue personally and it is something we will return to later in this book. It is most important to remember above all else that the goal of this work is not to *exclude* boys from STEM, but to *include* girls. In order to make sure girls are included and have equal access to STEM, we need to focus on strategies and tools to capture their attention and interest on par with that of boys. That being said, all of the activities, tools, and curricular resources in this book can and should be used with children of any gender.

Many of the resources in this book focus on the importance of exposing girls to female STEM role models through the picture books, media, and the people they are around. We should keep in mind that it is just as important for young boys to see these powerful and brilliant women in STEM as it is for girls. We want to shape the experiences young boys have too, so that they also grow up without stereotyped views of women's abilities.

If you are a female parent, educator, or caregiver, the way you model your personal attitudes and behaviors toward STEM is just as important around boys as it is around girls. It is important for young boys to see their female caregivers *negating* rather than *reinforcing* gender stereotypes about women in STEM. Therefore, the role-modeling strategies presented throughout this book are just as useful for those who work with boys as they are for those who work with girls.

Our focus should be creating a future where children of any gender can work creatively and collaboratively. In order to do so, we need to begin breaking gender stereotypes early and creating inclusive attitudes, not just with girls but with *all* children. If boys question why there is such a focus on girls right now, it is perfectly appropriate to explain that historically, girls have not had the same resources and access to STEM as boys. Engaging boys in conversation and action is an important piece of making lasting change.

THE PROBLEM IS NOT JUST FOR WOMEN

In this book I focus on the gender inequity of women in STEM, and I focus on reaching girls beginning in early childhood to address this inequity. But I cannot write a book about inequity in STEM without addressing the fact that women are not the only group underrepresented in STEM fields. According to the National Science Foundation, white men constitute approximately half of the scientists and engineers employed in science and engineering occupations. Asians are also highly represented in STEM, with Asian men making up 14% and Asian women making up 7% of the science and engineering workforce (National Science Foundation, 2017).

However, a peek behind the numbers tells a more nuanced story. A report by the Ascend Foundation found that Asians are the *least* likely to be promoted to managerial or executive positions, despite being the largest minority group of professionals and the most likely to be hired (Gee & Peck, 2017). In particular, Asian women are the least represented group as executives, at 66% underrepresentation (Gee & Peck, 2017). White men and women are twice as likely as Asians to become executives and hold almost three times the number of executive jobs (Gee & Peck, 2017).

Black and Hispanic men *and* women are drastically underrepresented in science and engineering fields. While Hispanic people make up a substantial component of the U.S. workforce (16%), they make up only 6% of the science and engineering workforce. Black men and women represent only 5% of the science and engineering workforce. Among all racial and ethnic groups, more men than women work in science and engineering occupations (National Science Foundation, 2017).

For women who are also minorities, the issues become more complicated. Ascend executive advisor Denise Peck summarizes these issues saying, "Minority women continue to bump against a double-paned glass ceiling. The data show that a general focus on developing women leaders has not addressed the distinct challenges for Asian, Black, or Hispanic women. This has been an unspoken truth in the minority community" (Ascend Team, 2017).

Research, but more importantly interventions and programs that make a real and lasting change, are needed to address the inequity among all groups underrepresented or experiencing bias and discrimination in STEM fields. It is beyond the scope of this book to address all areas of inequity in STEM, but it takes one small step by addressing the issues facing women and girls. We have quite a way to go in order to address all the inequities facing all people underrepresented in STEM fields.

A TIME FOR CHANGE

At its heart, the issue of girls and women in STEM is an ethical issue that must be addressed. It is an issue of access, equity, and fairness. The good news is there is a lot that we as educators and parents can do to make a difference.

Let's think back to that first stereotype we discussed—the stereotype of a male introvert, hunched over a computer, coding in solitude. It's time to rewrite that stereotype and show children that people who work in STEM are creative. They can be social. They can be any gender or race. By providing young children with positive messages, role models, and a range of educational experiences, adults can encourage children to persist in the face of negative (and false!) stereotypes.

Throughout this book we will educate ourselves on the state of the gender disparity in STEM fields; we will learn about the impact of stereotypes on the choices children and adults make; and we will explore the many ways we can combat these stereotypes every day. Together we can make simple changes in order to raise children who will be less likely to perpetuate gender stereotypes, breaking the cycle of bias once and for all.

REFERENCES

Ascend Team. (2017, October 11). *New research report from Ascend Foundation on Silicon Valley leadership diversity.* Retrieved from https://www.ascendleadership.org/news/369626/www.ascendleadership.org/research

Chemaly, S. (2016, March 16). The problem with a technology revolution designed primarily for men. *Quartz.* Retrieved from https://qz.com/640302/why-is-so-much-of-our-new-technology-designed-primarily-for-men/

Corbett, C., & Hill, C. (2015). *Solving the equation: The variables for women's success in engineering and computing.* Washington, DC: American Association of University Women.

Doerschuk, P., Liu, J., & Mann, J. (2007). Pilot summer camps in computing for middle school girls. *ACM SIGCSE Bulletin, 39*(3), 4. doi:10.1145/1269900.1268789

Duhaime-Ross, A. (2014, September 25). Apple promised an expansive health app, so why can't I track menstruation? *The Verge.* Retrieved from https://www.theverge.com/2014/9/25/6844021/apple-promised-an-expansive-health-app-so-why-cant-i-track

Gal-Ezer, J., & Stephenson, C. (2009). The current state of computer science in US high schools: A report from two national surveys. *Journal for Computing Teachers, 1,* 1–5.

Gee, B., & Peck, D. (2017). *The illusion of Asian success: Scant progress for minorities cracking the glass ceiling from 2007–2015.* Ascend Pan-Asian Leaders. Retrieved from https://c.ymcdn.com/sites/www.ascendleadership.org/resource/resmgr/research/TheIllusionofAsianSuccess.pdf

Hunt, V., Layton, D., & Prince, S. (2015). *Diversity matters.* McKinsey & Company. Retrieved from https://assets.mckinsey.com/~/media/857F440109AA4D13A54D9C496D86ED58.ashx

Hunt, V., Prince, S., Dixon-Fyle, S., Yee, L. (2017). *Delivering through diversity.* McKinsey & Company. Retrieved from https://www.mckinsey.com/~/media/mckinsey/business%20functions/organization/our%20insights/delivering%20through%20diversity/delivering-through-diversity_full-report.ashx

Miner, A. S., Milstein, A., Schueller, S., Hegde, R., Mangurian, C., & Linos, E. (2016). Smartphone-based conversational agents and responses to questions about mental health, interpersonal violence, and physical health. *JAMA Internal Medicine, 176*(5), 619–625.

National Science Foundation. (2017). *Women, minorities, and persons with disabilities in science and engineering: 2017.* Special Report NSF 17-310. Arlington, VA: National Center for Science and Engineering Statistics. Retrieved from https://www.nsf.gov/statistics/2017/nsf17310/

Ryan, E. G. (2013, November 8). Smartphones are made for giant man-hands. *Jezebel.* Retrieved from https://jezebel.com/smartphones-are-made-for-giant-man-hands-1461122433

Spencer, S. J., Steele, C. M., & Quinn, D. M. (1999). Stereotype threat and women's math performance. *Journal of Experimental Social Psychology, 35,* 4–28.

Steele, C. M. (1997). A threat in the air: How stereotypes shape intellectual identity and performance. *American Psychologist, 52*, 613–629.

Tufekci, Z. (2013, November 4). It's a man's phone. *Medium.* Retrieved from https://medium.com/technology-and-society/its-a-mans-phone-a26c6bee1b69

Williams, G. (2014). Are you sure your software is gender-neutral? *Interactions, 21*(1), 36–39. doi:10.1145/2524808

Part I

The Great Gender Divide in STEM

1

ENGAGING GIRLS WITH STEM BEFORE SECOND GRADE MAKES A DIFFERENCE

Today is Clara's birthday, and she is so excited to be turning seven! Several friends from her first-grade class at school have come to her house for a big party. Clara is opening her presents, squealing with delight as she excitedly unwraps the many dolls, treats, and books people have brought her. She gets to a large box from her friend Lindsay and shakes it next to her ear before ripping off the wrapping paper, trying to guess what could be inside. She sees a LEGO building kit and cannot hide her disappointment.

*"Lindsay, why did you get me a **boy's** toy?" Clara exclaims, confused. Before Lindsay can reply, Clara's mom interrupts embarrassed, "Is that a nice thing to say to your friend? Tell her thank you for the gift." Clara apologizes and thanks Lindsay for the LEGO set.*

*Over the next year, the LEGO set sits in Clara's playroom unused, save for the times she sits next to her dad, attentively watching **him** follow instructions from the box and assembling the house and car inside. Clara's dad loves tinkering with LEGOs; it's nostalgic for him. He's happy that Clara has a toy that he can enjoy exploring with her. He works proudly as Clara snuggles next to him, watching, but not building herself.*

Many educators, researchers, and parents are familiar with this scenario and have met and seen many "Claras" over the years. You may have encountered an incident like this at a birthday party, Christmas party, or another celebration where you've heard exchanges like this one between Clara, Lindsay, and her mom. A girl receives a "boy toy" or a boy receives a "girl toy." Or, a child simply receives a gift he or she may have no interest in using. Parents often swoop in to correct a social faux pas rather than discussing their child's reaction and where it came from. The party moves on and the item in question is typically returned, exchanged, or sits collecting dust on a shelf.

Clara's reaction may also have us asking questions about the LEGO set itself. What did the box look like to elicit such a strong reaction from Clara? How was it marketed? What color were the pieces? As you venture down even the most modern toy stores and bookstores, let alone larger department stores, you'll still be confronted by the division of the "pink aisle" and the "blue aisle."

It is clear that companies like LEGO create and market building sets for boys *and* for girls. Until the launch of the new "LEGO Friends" line in 2012), 90% of LEGO consumers were male (Ulaby, 2013). The new sets were distinctly characterized by pink and purple packaging and detailed mini-doll figures. Sales to girls tripled in the year this line was released (Ulaby, 2013). These new products give researchers and educators mixed feelings, and pose the question: Why do girls need *special* LEGOs? Why are "regular" LEGOs still seen as something "for boys"? Does any of that really matter as long as girls are now building and designing?

In Clara's case, the story continues beyond receiving the LEGO set. Instead of simply collecting dust in her playroom, the LEGO set makes another appearance when her father attempts to engage in some quality LEGO engineering time with her. The problem? Clara never lifts a finger! Once again, this problem is endemic among many parents and their children. Well-intentioned parents take the learning right out of their children's hands (literally) when engaging in building and experimenting projects at home, especially with toys like LEGOs. They are so excited to play with the set that they take on the role of engineer while their child takes on the role of spectator.

In this example, we face an even more serious problem. A young girl, who clearly admires and enjoys spending time with her father, sees him reinforcing a gender stereotype that she already holds: males are builders and engineers, and females are not. LEGOs are for boys and not for girls. She watches him build and is never encouraged to build or experiment with the set herself. While she and her father still share a tender moment together, a critical opportunity to instill confidence in her STEM skills is missed.

Research has shown that building and tinkering during one's childhood is beneficial in engineering careers later in life, and that women often have much less experience with childhood tinkering compared to their male counterparts (McIlwee & Robinson, 1992). In a seemingly harmless interaction with her father, Clara missed out on what could have been an opportunity to engage in tinkering and building herself.

Throughout this book, we will explore the many themes presented in the story of Clara's seventh birthday party. We will explore *why* so many young children gain the notion that certain toys, especially STEM-themed toys, are made for boys and not made for girls. We'll explore *how* parents, guardians, and teachers can foster important conversations around gender and STEM with their young children. We'll also take a peek into the world of media and advertising and its impact on girls. Finally, we'll explore the tools, toys, games, and activities that can engage girls (and all children, for that matter!) with STEM content in a hands-on and playful way that is developmentally appropriate for young children.

You may still be wondering why we've begun with the vignette of a seven-year-old's birthday party. If we want to reduce the gender divide between men and women in STEM fields, why aren't we concentrating on the high school or college "pre-career" years? You are not wrong to ask this question. In fact, there are a growing number of organizations and programs that *do* focus on supporting girls and young women in STEM pursuits during their adolescent and adult years. For example, Girls Who Code is a nonprofit organization that aims to support and increase the number of women in computer science through after-school clubs and summer programs for girls in middle and high school.

In addition to the well-known Girls Who Code, there are several other organizations aiming for public awareness outside of research and education circles. Kode with Klossy, founded by supermodel Karlie Kloss, has been bringing the issue of women in STEM to center stage in the pop-culture world. Kloss's organization has the goal of introducing teenage girls (ages 13–18) to coding through free coding summer camps and career scholarships. The AP STEM Access Program, launched in 2013, has enabled 320 public high schools across the country to start more than 500 new Advance Placement math, science, and computer science courses, and to encourage traditionally underrepresented minority and female students to enroll in and explore STEM courses and related careers.

Programs such as these are critical to increasing the presence of women in STEM in college and the career world. However, while high school and college are critical times to *continue* supporting young women in their pursuits of STEM careers, interventions that *begin* in adolescence are beginning too late for so many girls, like Clara, who have already formed stereotypes and beliefs about their interests and abilities.

Basic stereotypes begin to develop in children around two to three years of age (Kuhn, Nash, & Brucken, 1978; Signorella, Bigler, & Liben, 1993). Children generally develop the ability to label gender groups and to use gender labels in their speech between 18 and 24 months (Zosuls et al., 2009). Experimental studies have shown that young children are often quick to jump to conclusions about sex differences, even based on just *one* experience (Bauer & Coyne, 1997).

As children grow older, stereotypes about sports, occupations, and adult roles expand, and their gender associations grow increasingly sophisticated (Sinno & Killen, 2009). For example, children may go from making associations such as "boys like trucks" during preschool and kindergarten to associations like "trucks and airplanes are masculine" at around age eight (Martin & Ruble, 2004). In Clara's case, she has gone from the early association of "boys like LEGOs" and moved on to a more complex belief that "LEGOs are masculine." These associations may begin to impact children's decisions about what they are interested in, what they are good at, and what types of activities they should pursue.

Many researchers have theorized that a phenomenon known as "stereotype threat" explains why women and girls underperform in STEM fields. Stereotype threat refers to anxiety over the perception that one's performance on a task or activity will be seen through the lens of a negative stereotype (Spencer, Steele, & Quinn, 1999; Steele, 1997). Studies have shown that invoking or calling attention to a stereotype can impact performance on tasks. For example, telling a woman that women do not perform as well as men on math tasks (i.e., invoking the stereotype that women aren't good at math) will lead to reduced performance on a math test (Spencer, Steele, & Quinn, 1999). In part

II of this book, we will deeply explore the role of stereotypes and stereotype threat on the way women and girls perform on STEM tasks and shape their experiences with STEM.

So what can we do to combat the development of these negative stereotypes? The first step is to start early. We should begin by reaching kids while they are in their foundational early childhood years: around ages four to seven, or approximately pre-kindergarten through second grade. Throughout this book, when we talk about "young children" or "early childhood," this is the age range we should be thinking about. Past work has shown that from an economic and a developmental standpoint, educational interventions that begin in early childhood are associated with lower costs and more durable effects than interventions that begin later on (e.g., Cunha & Heckman, 2007).

Two commonly cited reports, the National Research Council's *Eager to Learn* (2000) and the Institute of Medicine's *From Neurons to Neighborhoods* (2000), reinforce the importance of early experiences for later school achievement. Where STEM is concerned, research suggests that children who are exposed to STEM curriculum and programming at an early age demonstrate fewer gender-based stereotypes regarding STEM careers (Metz, 2007; Steele, 1997) and fewer obstacles entering these fields later in life (Madill et al., 2007; Markert, 1996).

What do STEM initiatives in early childhood settings look like? Historically, early childhood STEM education has focused on building foundational numeracy skills (math, the "M" in STEM) and an understanding of the natural sciences including plants, animals, and the weather (science, the "S" of STEM). Meanwhile, technology and engineering (the "T" and "E"), as well as other aspects of science, are often missing (Bers, 2008; Bers, Seddighin, & Sullivan, 2013). This is a major issue, as we will see in chapter 4, because it is in the technical STEM fields, including engineering and computer science, where women are most drastically underrepresented.

Recently, there has been a growing national-level discussion around STEM, and the question of how to teach technology and engineering has become a pressing issue across a growing number of countries (U.K. Department of Education, 2013; U.S. Department of Education, 2010). New education policy changes, commercial products, and nonprofit organizations are promoting a message that highlights the benefits of computational thinking (i.e., skills often associated with computing that include problem-solving, design, and systematic analysis), digital citizenship (i.e., being able to effectively use digital technology, especially in order to participate responsibly in social and civic activities), and technological literacy (i.e., the ability to effectively use technology to access, manage, evaluate, create, and communicate information), even for our youngest learners (Bers, 2012; Hobbs, 2010; Hollandsworth, Dowdy, & Donovan, 2011; White House, 2011; Wing, 2006). These initiatives have led to the creation of many wonderful programs and tools that can be used to engage young children in the world of technology and engineering, and STEM in general. We will take a look at some of these tools in part III of this book.

NATURAL SCIENTISTS AND ENGINEERS

Adults may be surprised at what very young children can accomplish when given developmentally appropriate STEM tools to explore. For example, children as young as four years old can successfully build and program a simple robot and learn concepts of engineering design (Bers, Ponte, Juelich, Viera, & Schenker, 2002; Cejka, Rogers, & Portsmore, 2006; Perlman, 1976; Sullivan, Kazakoff, & Bers, 2013; Wyeth, 2008). Engineering and computer programming in early childhood education can be used to explore a range of interdisciplinary projects across STEM fields, but perhaps more importantly, it can foster the development of cognitive and social skills that are important for young children to practice.

Early studies with the text-based programming language LOGO have demonstrated that computer programming can help young children with number sense, language skills, and visual memory (Clements, 1999). New developmentally appropriate technological materials have evolved in the tradition of educational manipulatives like Froebel's "gifts," Montessori materials, and Nicholson's loose parts. Like the tools that came before them, these new technologies can help children develop a stronger understanding of mathematical concepts such as number, size, and shape in much the same way that traditional manipulatives like pattern blocks, beads, and balls do (Brosterman, 1997; Resnick et al., 1998).

Programmable robotics kits are an example of a digital tool that has been shown to increase girls' level of interest in being an engineer when they grow up. Early childhood initiatives with robotics also increase the percentage of kids (both boys and girls) who view robotics as gender-neutral rather than "for boys" or "for girls" (Sullivan, 2016).

But let's forget about the research and the products for just a moment and think about what we inherently know about young children. When parents and teachers ask why they should focus on young children and STEM, the easiest answer is, "it's just a good time." And it's true. Early childhood is a unique time in development characterized by curiosity, inquiry, and playfulness.

Anyone who has worked with five-year-olds, for example, has heard them ask endless "why" questions as they grapple to make sense of the world around them. Young children are natural scientists, coming up with theories about how the world around them works. They are mathematicians, counting, exploring shapes, and exploring concepts of size and depth. They are engineers and explorers: they build, stack, design, and redesign. Today's young children are also naturally curious about the digital technology that surrounds them, and they often wonder how their tablets and televisions work. They are exposed to a human-engineered environment every time they walk through automatically opening and closing doors and place their hands under a water faucet that automatically provides water.

As adults, we do not often question why our environment works the way it does. But a five-year-old genuinely wants to know *why* the sky is blue. She genuinely wants to know *how* a water faucet can "know" your hands are underneath it. Young children are hungry to understand the big world around them. It is critical to engage young children while they are curious about the things they see and observe. We must not dismiss their questions about the world—even when we as adults do not know the answers! When we do not know how to respond to children's questions, it is the perfect time to model our own sense of scientific inquiry, make hypotheses, and try to uncover answers together.

MAKING CHANGES IN EARLY EDUCATION

Some parts of this book will focus on designing activities that are tailored to formal education settings such as schools and daycare centers, as well as informal education settings such as clubs, camps, and museums. But it is important for parents to remember that while school-based initiatives are critical, they cannot solely rely only on what teachers are doing in school. Many scholars have found that the home environment can strongly influence the interests and personal goals of children (e.g., Bell, Lewenstein, Shouse, & Feder, 2009; Crowley & Jacobs, 2002). When it comes to a girl's developing interest and ideas about STEM, the role modeling of parents and parental expectation about ability and interest can change how girls see themselves (Margolis & Fisher, 2002). This was clear in the vignette about Clara, her father, and her mother.

After considering *why* early childhood matters, the latter chapters in this book will explore *how* you can engage girls in integrative STEM projects and activities, beginning in pre-kindergarten. We will learn strategies for designing school and home activities, and selecting the games, kits, and apps that will be sure to engage girls during their pivotal early childhood years, setting them up for long-term success. Most importantly, we will look at our own practices as parents and educators and think about how we can avoid the often overlooked mistakes that well-meaning adults tend to make.

Before we can make effective change in our own work, it is important to reflect on where we are currently in our beliefs and practices. Table 1.1 provides a simple checklist for adults to begin thinking about everyday things we can be doing with young children. If you answered "regularly" to most of the questions in this checklist, you are probably already engaging all children, including girls, with quality STEM education practices. You will be interested in learning about new technologies, project ideas, and approaches to curricula to complement your current STEM education philosophy. If you answered "never" or "sometimes" to most of the questions, do not fear! You are ready to begin gaining the knowledge, confidence, and skills you need to create powerful experiences for young girls by the time you finish reading this book.

Early exposure to STEM allows girls to imagine and dream about a whole range of possible careers they might have when they grow up, including astronaut, architect, electrical engineer, and computer programmer. But whether the girls we teach today grow up to be engineers and scientists or something completely unrelated to STEM, early exposure to these concepts will provide them with problem-solving skills, a sense of creativity, and self-confidence that will be useful in any domain they choose. It is never too early for us as educators to show girls all the possibilities the world has in store for them.

Table 1.1. Checklist: How Often Do I Engage in Best Practices for Engaging Girls in STEM?

Check the appropriate column (Regularly, Sometimes, or Never) for each statement. Remember, "I" refers to YOU and your practices with your students/kids, not a science teacher, spouse, or other specialist.

	Regularly	Sometimes	Never
I read aloud books that feature girls and women engaging in science, technology, engineering, and mathematics.	☐	☐	☐
I expose young children to diverse role models from STEM fields, including women and minorities.	☐	☐	☐
I explore hands-on science and math experiments with young children.	☐	☐	☐
I expose young children to novel technologies such as robotics kits and programming languages.	☐	☐	☐
I encourage all young children to play with building- and engineering-focused manipulatives such as blocks and LEGOs.	☐	☐	☐
I model my own sense of scientific inquiry about the world around me.	☐	☐	☐
I am open to having conversations about gender roles and stereotypes when children express an interest.	☐	☐	☐
I encourage young children to discover ways to figure out problems and solutions themselves, rather than asking an adult.	☐	☐	☐

REFERENCES

Bauer, P. J., & Coyne, M. J. (1997). When the name says it all: Preschoolers' recognition and use of the gendered nature of common proper names. *Social Development, 6*, 271–291.

Bell, P., Lewenstein, B., Shouse, A. W., & Feder, M. A. (2009). *Learning science in informal environments: People, places, and pursuits* (Vol. 32, No. 3, p. 127). Washington, DC: National Academies Press.

Bers, M. U. (2008). *Blocks, robots and computers: Learning about technology in early childhood.* New York: Teacher's College Press.

Bers, M. U. (2012). *Designing digital experiences for positive youth development: From playpen to playground.* Oxford: Oxford University Press.

Bers, M. U., Ponte, I., Juelich, K., Viera, A., & Schenker, J. (2002). Teachers as designers: Integrating robotics into early childhood education. *Information Technology in Childhood Education Annual, 2002*(1), 123–145.

Bers, M. U., Seddighin, S., & Sullivan, A. (2013). Ready for robotics: Bringing together the T and E of STEM in early childhood teacher education. *Journal of Technology and Teacher Education, 21*(3), 355–377.

Brosterman, N. (1997). *Inventing kindergarten.* New York: H. N. Abrams.

Cejka, E., Rogers, C., & Portsmore, M. (2006). Kindergarten robotics: Using robotics to motivate math, science, and engineering literacy in elementary school. *International Journal of Engineering Education, 22*(4), 711–722.

Clements, D. H. (1999). Young children and technology. In *Dialogue on early childhood science, mathematics, and technology education.* Washington, DC: American Association for the Advancement of Science.

Crowley, K., & Jacobs, M. (2002). Building islands of expertise in everyday family activity. In G. Leinhardt, K. Crowley, & K. Knutson (Eds.), *Learning conversations in museums* (pp. 333–356). Mahwah, NJ: Lawrence Erlbaum Associates.

Cunha, F. & Heckman, J. (2007). The technology of skill formation. *American Economic Review, 97*(2), 31–47.

Hobbs, R. (2010). *Digital and media literacy: A plan of action.* Aspen Institute and the Knight Foundation. Retrieved from https://kf-site-production.s3.amazonaws.com/publications/pdfs/000/000/075/original/Digital_and_Media_Literacy_A_Plan_of_Action.pdf

Hollandsworth, R., Dowdy, L., & Donovan, J. (2011). Digital citizenship in K–12: It takes a village. *TechTrends, 55*(4), 37–47.

Institute of Medicine. (2000). *From neurons to neighborhoods: The science of early childhood development.* Washington, DC: National Academies Press. https://doi.org/10.17226/9824

Kuhn, D., Nash, S. C., & Brucken, L. (1978). Sex role concepts of two- and three-year-olds. *Child Development, 49*, 445–51.

Madill, H., Campbell, R. G., Cullen, D. M., Armour, M. A., Einsiedel, A. A., Ciccocioppo, A. L., & Coffin, W. L. (2007). Developing career commitment in STEM-related fields: Myth versus reality. In R. J. Burke, M. C. Mattis, & E. Elgar (Eds.), *Women and minorities in science, technology, engineering and mathematics: Upping the numbers* (pp. 210–244). Northhampton, MA: Edward Elgar Publishing.

Margolis, J., & Fisher, A. (2002). *Unlocking the clubhouse: Women in computing.* Cambridge, MA: MIT Press.

Markert, L. R. (1996). Gender related to success in science and technology. *Journal of Technology Studies, 22*(2), 21–29.

Martin, C. L., & Ruble, D. N. (2004). Children's search for gender cues: Cognitive perspectives on gender development. *Current Directions in Psychological Science, 13*, 67–70.

McIlwee, J. S., & Robinson, J. G. (1992). *Women in engineering: Gender, power, and workplace culture.* SUNY Press.

Metz, S. S. (2007). Attracting the engineering of 2020 today. In R. Burke and M. Mattis (Eds.), *Women and minorities in science, technology, engineering and mathematics: Upping the numbers* (pp. 184–209). Northampton, MA: Edward Elgar Publishing.

National Research Council. (2000). *Eager to learn: Educating our preschoolers*. Washington, DC: National Academies Press. https://doi.org/10.17226/9745.

Perlman, R. (1976). *Using computer technology to provide a creative learning environment for preschool children* [Logo memo no. 24]. Cambridge, MA: MIT Artificial Intelligence Laboratory Publications 260.

Resnick, M., Martin, F., Berg, R., Borovoy, R., Colella, V., Kramer, K., & Silverman, B. (1998, April). Digital manipulatives. *Proceedings of the SIGCHI Conference on Human Factors in Computing Systems, Los Angeles*, pp. 281–287.

Signorella, M. L., Bigler, R. S., & Liben, L. S. (1993). Developmental differences in children's gender schemata about others: A meta-analytic review. *Development Review, 13*(2), 147–183.

Sinno, S. M., & Killen, M. (2009). Moms at work and dads at home: children's evaluations of parental roles. *Applied Developmental Science, 13*(1),16–29.

Spencer, S. J., Steele, C. M., & Quinn, D. M. (1999). Stereotype threat and women's math performance. *Journal of Experimental Social Psychology, 35*, 4–28.

Steele, C. M. (1997). A threat in the air: How stereotypes shape intellectual identity and performance. *American Psychologist, 52*, 613–629.

Sullivan, A. (2016). *Breaking the STEM stereotype: Investigating the use of robotics to change young children's gender stereotypes about technology and engineering*. Unpublished doctoral dissertation, Tufts University, Medford, MA.

Sullivan, A., Kazakoff, E. R., & Bers, M. U. (2013). The wheels on the bot go round and round: Robotics curriculum in pre-kindergarten. *Journal of Information Technology Education: Innovations in Practice, 12*, 203–219.

U.K. Department for Education. (2013). The National Curriculum in England: Framework document. London: The Stationery Office.

Ulaby, N. (2013). Girls' Legos are a hit, but why do girls need special Legos? *NPR: Weekend Edition Saturday*.

U.S. Department of Education, Office of Educational Technology. (2010). Transforming American education: Learning powered by technology. Draft National Educational Technology Plan 2010. Washington, DC: 2010.

White House. (2011). Educate to innovate. Retrieved from http://www.whitehouse.gov/issues/education/ educate-innovate

Wing, J. M. (2006). Computational thinking. *Communications of the ACM, 49*(3), 33–35.

Wyeth, P. (2008). How young children learn to program with sensor, action, and logic blocks. *International Journal of the Learning Sciences, 17*(4), 517–550.

Zosuls, K. M., Ruble, D. N., Tamis-LeMonda, C. S., Shrout, P. E., Bornstein, M. H., & Greulich, F. K. (2009). The acquisition of gender labels in infancy: Implications for sex-typed play. *Developmental Psychology, 45*(3), 688–701.

2

CRUSH THE "GIRLS ARE BAD AT MATH" MYTH

DEFINING STEM

Thus far, we have been talking about STEM (Science, Technology, Engineering, Mathematics) disciplines grouped together—and we will return to doing so for the majority of the second and third parts of this book. The reason for this is simple: STEM education is at its core an *interdisciplinary* approach to education. We can define STEM as an approach to learning in which interdisciplinary academic concepts come together with real-world lessons, encouraging students to apply science, technology, engineering, and mathematics in a variety of meaningful contexts.

While some may still consider STEM in terms of segregated subjects, most modern educators understand that it is hard to study domains such as engineering without *also* applying mathematical skills, for example. We see that these fields have a great deal of overlap and work hand in hand with one another. We know that multiple aspects of STEM can often be explored together, especially at the early childhood level. Children can explore counting and numeracy while creating a computer program. They can employ the scientific method while exploring engineering. The possibilities for authentic overlap are endless. Furthermore, there is a need for STEM coursework to mirror professional practices and careers, which typically include the integration of two or more STEM fields as well as the ability to problem-solve and collaborate with others across many disciplines (including the arts), and to think critically in order to solve societal issues and address human dilemmas.

However, it is crucial for us to momentarily tease apart the individual components of STEM to see how girls and women are progressing in each STEM domain. Not all STEM fields are created equally, and in fact, there are many STEM areas in which the representation of women is equal to or even surpasses the representation of men. This chapter looks at the experiences of girls and women in the "M" (mathematics) fields of STEM. Chapter 3 will look at the "S" (science), and chapter 4 will explore the "T" (Technology) and "E" (engineering) fields.

WOMEN IN MATHEMATICS FIELDS

Have you ever heard any of the following statements? Have you ever said one of them?

Girls are bad at math.
Women can't do math.
Men are better at math.
Boys are naturally good at math and girls are naturally good at reading.
I can't figure that out because I'm a girl.

Most girls and women have heard (or said) at least one of these statements at some point in their lives. Of all the STEM domains, mathematics is potentially the field most laden with long-standing stereotypes about the abilities of males and females. For decades, there has been a running commentary in our society that mathematics is a naturally masculine ability. Statements like the ones above are commonplace at home and at school. They come out of the mouths of children and adults of all genders. Because mathematics ability is also at the core of many fields, including technology and engineering domains, negative experiences or attitudes toward math can eliminate a whole range of courses, extracurricular activities, and potential careers for students. Therefore, it is important to look closely at the experiences of girls and women in mathematics fields.

Women's representation in mathematics and statistics has reached more than 40% at the bachelor and master degree levels (National Science Foundation, 2017). But at higher levels of education, we see a greater divide, with female representation in mathematics at the doctoral level remaining below 30% (National Science Foundation, 2017). When it comes to faculty positions in mathematics, we see an even greater gender disparity, with just 15% of tenure-track positions in mathematics held by women (Hu, 2016).

MATHEMATICS DURING THE K–12 YEARS

Clearly men are outnumbering women at the highest level of mathematics education and professions. So, when does this divide begin to appear? And are there differences in *performance* in math areas based on gender, or simply less women *interested* in pursuing mathematics professionally? According to research over the past decade, there are generally no longer differences in average math performance between girls and boys in the general school population (Hyde, Lindberg, Linn, Ellis, & Williams 2008). During the early elementary years, research suggests that girls perform at least as well (and sometimes better) than boys in mathematics (Hyde & Linn, 2006).

When it comes to *attitudes* toward mathematics, though, there are differences that begin to emerge as early as elementary school. Research suggests that boys are generally more interested in math than are girls (Frenzel, Pekrun, & Goetz, 2007; Köller, Baumert, & Schnabel, 2001; Watt, 2004). Some research also shows that girls are less confident in their math abilities than boys (Else-Quest, Hyde, & Linn, 2010; Herbert & Stipek, 2005; Hyde et al., 2008).

On the flip side, there has also been notable concern about boys' reading achievement in elementary school—a domain in which girls have historically outperformed boys. In recent years, concerns about boys' reading skills have taken some attention away from girls and math at the early childhood and elementary level. However, it is important to consider that the reading gender gap, which favors girls, *narrows* during the elementary grades (Robinson & Lubienski, 2011), whereas the gender gap in math that favors boys *grows* during elementary school (Gibbs, 2010). This indicates that math may be an area where teachers, parents, and researchers still need to devote increased attention beginning at the early childhood level.

Gender differences in math performance are critical to look at during the adolescent years as well. In high school, female and male students earn an equal number of math and science credits, and females tend to receive higher average grades than males (Shettle et al., 2007). However, looking at high-stakes math tests commonly taken by high school students (such as the SAT and the ACT) paints a slightly different picture. Here we see that, while female students' performance on these tests have improved over the years, male students still outperform female students on tests like the SAT (College Board S.A.T., 2016).

Gender differences on math tests tend to be more pronounced when the test is less related to specific material that is taught in school. For example, gender differences are more pronounced on a general test like the SAT math test as opposed to a math test given in class covering specific curriculum content (Catsambis, 1994, Pomerantz, Altermatt, & Saxon, 2002, Willingham & Cole, 1997).

GENDER DIFFERENCES IN MATH PERFORMANCE EXPLAINED

What are the root causes of these gender differences? Are men really better than women at certain aspects of mathematics? There is a long-standing stereotype that men, by nature, have better spatial reasoning skills than women. This stereotype has persisted in part because women have been shown to underperform on complex mathematical problem-solving and standardized tests involving spatial reasoning and mental rotation (Hyde, 2014; Lindberg, Hyde, Petersen, & Linn, 2010; Miller & Halpern, 2014). However, there is no scientific basis to support the stereotype that genetic or hormonal differences between men and women can explain major gender differences in spatial reasoning (Assessing Women in Engineering Project, 2005; Hoffman, Gneezy, & List, 2011). In other words: being a girl does *not* mean you are innately less capable at math.

If biology is not at the root of the differences, then what is? This is a complicated question with complicated answers. Although there may be many explanations, this book focuses specifically on the powerful role of stereotypes and societal influences on women's attitudes, confidence, and abilities in STEM fields like mathematics. While some research has found that boys are more interested in math, it is important to point out that our attitudes, interests, and beliefs are significantly shaped by the culture we live in and the experiences we have growing up. Attitudes are important predictors of math performance and math-related career choices. Therefore, it is important for adults to think about providing girls with exciting and engaging math experiences beginning in early childhood.

CRUSHING STEREOTYPES ABOUT GIRLS AND MATH

Clearly, there is a need to address the pervasive stereotypes about girls and math that have become a big part of our culture. Part II of this book will delve deeply into the research behind stereotypes and the harmful impact they can have on women's performance on high-stakes math tests like the SAT. In the meantime, is important to point out that skills like spatial reasoning are malleable, and research has shown that spatial reasoning abilities can be improved through practice. As we will see later in this book when we explore the growth mindset, an important mediator for supporting girls in mathematics is to remind them that no one has a skill or ability just "by nature," and certainly not simply by being male, female, or any gender. Hard work, practice, and perseverance is what allows us to harness our skills and develop new abilities. Supporting this mindset is one of the most important things that adults can do to crush negative stereotypes about girls and math.

It is easy for adults to brush off minor gender differences in interest and performance in math as small or inconsequential at the early childhood and early elementary level. Remember that these small differences can grow to have a huge impact on children later on. Foundational math skills set the stage for countless opportunities children will be exposed to later in life. Researchers Ganley & Lubienski (2016, p. 190) put it best by saying, "math interventions for girls should begin where and when they are first detected—in elementary school—and not wait for middle and high school."

REFERENCES

Assessing Women in Engineering (AWE) Project. (2005). Cooperative learning. *AWE Research Overviews*. Retrieved from https://www.engr.psu.edu/awe/misc/ARPs/CooperativeLearning_03_17_08.pdf

Catsambis, S. (1994). The path to math: Gender and racial-ethnic differences in mathematics participation from middle school to high school. *Sociology of Education, 67*(3), 199–215. DOI: 10.2307/2112791

College Board: SAT. (2016). *College-bound seniors: Total group profile report*. New York, NY: The College Board.

Else-Quest, N. M., Hyde, J. S., & Linn, M. C. (2010). Cross-national patterns of gender differences in mathematics: A meta-analysis. *Psychological Bulletin, 136*(1), 103.

Frenzel, A. C., Pekrun, R., & Goetz, T. (2007). Girls and mathematics—A "hopeless" issue? A control-value approach to gender differences in emotions towards mathematics. *European Journal of Psychology of Education, 22*(4), 497.

Ganley, C. M., & Lubienski, S. T. (2016). Mathematics confidence, interest, and performance: Examining gender patterns and reciprocal relations. *Learning and Individual Differences, 47*, 182–193. https://doi.org/10.1016/j.lindif.2016.01.002

Gibbs, B. G. (2010). Reversing fortunes or content change? Gender gaps in math-related skill throughout childhood. *Social Science Research, 39*(4), 540–569.

Herbert, J., & Stipek, D. (2005). The emergence of gender differences in children's perceptions of their academic competence. *Journal of Applied Developmental Psychology, 26*(3), 276–295.

Hoffman, M., Gneezy, U., & List, J. A. (2011). Nurture affects gender differences in spatial abilities. *Proceedings of the National Academy of Sciences, 108*(36), 14786–14788. https://doi.org/10.1073/pnas.1015182108

Hu, J. (2016, November 4). Why are there so few women mathematicians? How a corrosive culture keeps women out of leadership positions on math journals. *The Atlantic*. Retrieved from https://www.theatlantic.com/science/archive/2016/11/math-women/506417/

Hyde, J. S. (2014). Gender similarities and differences. *Annual Review of Psychology, 65*, 373–398.

Hyde, J. S., & Linn, M. C. (2006). Gender similarities in mathematics and science. *Science, 314*(5799), 599–600.

Hyde, J. S., Lindberg, S. M., Linn, M. C., Ellis, A. B., & Williams, C. C. (2008). Gender similarities characterize math performance. *Science, 321*(5888), 494–495.

Köller, O., Baumert, J., & Schnabel, K. (2001). Does interest matter? The relationship between academic interest and achievement in mathematics. *Journal for Research in Mathematics Education, 32*(5), 448–470. DOI: 10.2307/749801

Lindberg, S. M., Hyde, J. S., Petersen, J. L., & Linn, M. C. (2010). New trends in gender and mathematics performance: a meta-analysis. *Psychological bulletin, 136*(6), 1123.

Miller, D. I., & Halpern, D. F. (2014). The new science of cognitive sex differences. *Trends in cognitive sciences, 18*(1), 37–45.

National Science Foundation. (2017). *Women, minorities, and persons with disabilities in science and engineering: 2017*. Special Report NSF 17-310. Arlington, VA: National Center for Science and Engineering Statistics. Retrieved from https://www.nsf.gov/statistics/2017/nsf17310/

Pomerantz, E. M., Altermatt, E. R., & Saxon, J. L. (2002). Making the grade but feeling distressed: Gender differences in academic performance and internal distress. *Journal of Educational Psychology, 94*(2), 396.

Robinson, J. P., & Lubienski, S. T. (2011). The development of gender achievement gaps in mathematics and reading during elementary and middle school: Examining direct cognitive assessments and teacher ratings. *American Educational Research Journal, 48*(2), 268–302.

Shettle, C., Roey, S., Mordica, J., Perkins, R., Nord, C., Teodorovic, J., Lyons, M., Averett, C., Kastberg, D., & Brown, J. (2007). *The nation's report card: America's high school graduates*. NCES 2007-467. Washington, DC: National Center for Education Statistics.

Watt, H. M. (2004). Development of adolescents' self-perceptions, values, and task perceptions according to gender and domain in 7th- through 11th-grade Australian students.
Child Development, 75(5), 1556–1574.
Willingham, W. W., & Cole, N. S. (1997). *Gender and fair assessment.* Hillsdale, NJ: Lawrence Erlbaum.

3

CELEBRATE WOMEN IN SCIENCE

We saw in the previous chapter that men outnumber women at the highest levels of mathematics-related careers, and began to discuss the powerful role of negative stereotypes about women's mathematics aptitude. Shifting our focus to the sciences, we see a slightly different picture. When we remove the technical sciences such as computer science (don't worry—we will address these fields in the next chapter), we see that women have made substantial gains in many science disciplines.

In chemistry, for example, women made up only 8% of chemists in 1960 but accounted for 39% percent of the chemistry workforce by 2013 (Corbett & Hill, 2015). In the National Science Foundation's 2017 reporting of numbers, the proportion of women in the biosciences generally ranged between 51% and 58%, depending on the specific field and degree level (National Science Foundation, 2017). This means women account for approximately half (or more) of bioscience professionals. This is a huge leap forward for women in the sciences!

In the social sciences, recent statistics show that women are even *more* prevalent than men in many areas. For example, women are *more* likely than men to be employed as psychologists, a profession once dominated by men (National Science Foundation, 2017). Back in 1970, women only represented about 20% of PhD recipients in psychology (Cynkar, 2007). Now, women account for 70% or more of the graduates at each degree level of psychology, and men are in the minority in this field (National Science Foundation, 2017).

This may be due to the flexibility that seeing patients allows women, especially those balancing children and other responsibilities. Despite their numbers, however, women working in psychology typically earn 9% less than men (Cynkar, 2007). Moreover, within academia women represent only 25% of full professors in graduate departments of psychology, which is incredibly disproportionate to their representation of the field on a whole (Cynkar, 2007). If we are going to make a change, it is important to look beyond the numbers to the gender inequities that still persist within these fields.

MEDICAL SCIENCES

Outside of the social sciences, women struggle to climb to the highest ranks in many of the medical and laboratory sciences, even disciplines in which they appear to be well represented. Although women are *more* likely than men to work in many health-related occupations, they are *less* likely to work at the highest levels and in the most lucrative specialties such as physicians, surgeons, or dentists (National Science Foundation, 2017).

When looking at professors of surgery, for example, women make up only 8% of professors, 13% of associate professors, and 26% of assistant professors of surgery (Wolfe, 2018). This is reflective of the lack of female surgeons in general, with only 19.2% of females working as surgeons (Wolfe, 2018). In specialties like orthopedic surgery, women make up just 5% of the field (Association of American Medical Colleges, 2015). This indicates there is still be work to do *within* the field of medicine to ensure that women are equally represented in the highest positions.

BARRIERS AT THE HIGHEST LEVELS

While the number of women in scientific fields in general are growing, women continue to face challenges and often struggle to gain recognition, in comparison to men. In 2018, female physicist Donna Strickland won a Nobel Prize in physics for her work on generating high-intensity ultra-short optical pulses (a technique known as "chirped pulse amplification"). What came out of the media coverage for her award was the somewhat shocking revelation that Dr. Strickland was just the third female physicist to *ever* receive this award. She joined the slim ranks of female scientists Marie Curie, who received a Nobel in 1903, and Maria Goeppert-Mayer, who received one in 1963 (Feeney, 2018).

So why aren't more female scientists winning these prizes? Writer and ethics professor Mary Feeney writes about the powerful role of stereotypes, noting:

> All of us—the general public, the media, university employees, students and professors—have ideas of what a scientist and a Nobel Prize winner looks like. That image is predominantly male, white and older—which makes sense given 97 percent of the science Nobel Prize winners have been men. (Feeney, 2018)

While many science fields are already extremely demanding and competitive, women face added hurdles when climbing the ranks that men typically do not. From pay inequity to training and career lifestyles that do not always accommodate raising children (which still remains a female-dominated endeavor), women face many challenges that persist in these fields up to the highest levels. The added burden of a scientist stereotype that clashes with the way many girls and women see themselves prevents many from ever entering these fields.

THE MAD SCIENTIST STEREOTYPE

When we are asked to imagine a scientist, many of us right off the bat still picture a man with wild hair, a white lab coat, working in an isolated workspace in a manic frenzy. This might be due to the portrayal of iconic scientists in the media (is anyone aware that their vision of a scientist greatly resembles Doc Brown from *Back to the Future*?). The media often portrays scientists as eccentric and antisocial, working persistently at something only of personal interest to them. This stereotype can make the sciences seem off-putting for many people, and especially women and girls who tend to be drawn to more collaborative work environments.

It is time for an updated image of what a scientist looks like and what type of work they engage in. While iconic characters like Doc Brown or

Dr. Frankenstein are certainly compelling for people to read about or watch on-screen, children need to learn about real-world scientists who often engage in projects to help others, improve the environment, and more. Scientists who work collaboratively with others, both within and outside of their fields. Scientists who represent a range of genders, races, and backgrounds. This exposure should begin happening at the earliest exploration of science education.

SCIENCE EDUCATION

In order to continue growing the representation of women in the sciences, especially at the highest levels where men still dominate, changes must start during the early education years when girls receive their first introduction to the sciences. The goal of science education is to understand the natural world through a process known as scientific inquiry (Worth, 2010). Science helps us explain the world around us, such as seasons, animal behaviors, and what causes illnesses. The natural sciences are very much present in early childhood classrooms as children explore topics such as plants, animals, and the weather. But science education in school is (or should be) just as much about shaping children's positive attitudes toward science as it is about teaching specific scientific content.

When thinking about engaging girls in science, fostering positive attitudes can be just as important as actual scientific skills. Research has found a significant correlation between attitude and achievement in science (Steinkamp & Maehr, 1983). Beginning as early as elementary school, boys typically have more interest in science than girls (Clark, 1972; Clark & Nelson, 1972; Kotte, 1992). Girls also tend to participate less actively than boys in extracurricular science activities such as science competitions (Jones, 1991; Olson, 1985). Therefore, *during* the school day, beginning in early childhood, it is a critical for teachers to begin shaping children's attitudes toward science and providing girls with positive science experiences. It is also important for all children, regardless of gender, to develop positive attitudes toward science so that they grow up to be knowledgeable "scientific citizens" who are able to digest scientific topics in the news and are confident enough to engage in public discourse around scientific advancements and issues.

When looking at inequities in science education, socioeconomic status (SES) may be an important factor to consider—perhaps more so than gender. Children growing up in low-SES families typically receive fewer early opportunities to learn about the natural and social sciences, in part because their parents often have less science knowledge themselves. These families may also have fewer financial resources available to direct toward their children's educational development (Bradley & Corwyn, 2002; Hart & Risley, 1995; Sackes, Trundle, Bell, & O'Connell, 2011).

As the economic status of parents rises, so does their child's positive attitude toward science. For this reason, it is doubly crucial for the early childhood classroom to engage children in scientific inquiry and exploration of the natural world in order to ensure that *all* young children are developing positive attitudes toward science, regardless of their resources at home.

RECOGNIZING WOMEN IN SCIENCE

While learning about science, it is important for parents and educators to help children recognize and celebrate female scientists. In part II of this book, we will explore the importance of exposing girls (and boys, or children of any gender, for that matter) to female role models in the sciences. Rather than seeing these women as unique with unattainable achievements, it is important for young girls to see aspects of themselves in these scientists; to see women they can imagine growing up to be like.

From historical to present-day, real to fictional, there are plenty of amazing female scientists to present to girls. For example, in the same year Donna Strickland won the Nobel Prize in physics, biochemical engineer Frances Arnold won the Nobel Prize in chemistry. Women are making their mark in the sciences, and it is important to highlight and celebrate their achievements with young children. Chapter 8 will give you more examples of female scientists to become familiar with so that you can turn them into household names for the young children with whom you work or raise.

LOOKING AHEAD AT THE TECHNICAL SCIENCES

In the following chapter, we turn to the technical sciences and look at female representation in the "T" (technology) and "E" (engineering) fields of STEM. While we are seeing a high proportion of women in many of the social sciences and biosciences, when it comes to technology and engineering, the numbers are less uplifting. In the following chapter we'll explore why this might be the case, and what we can do about it.

REFERENCES

Association of American Medical Colleges. (2015). Active physicians by sex and specialty, 2015. *Physician Specialty Data Report*. Retrieved from https://www.aamc.org/data/workforce/reports/458712/1-3-chart.html

Bradley, R. H., & Corwyn, R. F. (2002). Socioeconomic status and child development. *Annual Review of Psychology, 53*(1), 371–399.

Clark, C. (1972). A determination of commonalities of science interests held by intermediate grade children in inner-city, suburban and rural schools. *Science Education, 56*, 125–136.

Clark, C., & Nelson, P. (1972). Commonalities of science interests held by intermediate grade children. *Journal of Education, 154*, 3–12.

Corbett, C., & Hill, C. (2015). *Solving the equation: The variables for women's success in engineering and computing*. Washington, DC: American Association of University Women.

Cynkar, A. (2007). The changing gender composition of psychology. *Monitor on Psychology, 38*(6), 46.

Feeney, M. (2018, October 5). Why more women don't win science Nobels. *The Conversation*. Retrieved from https://theconversation.com/why-more-women-dont-win-science-nobels-104370

Hart, B., & Risley, T. R. (1995). *Meaningful differences in the everyday experience of young American children*. Baltimore, MD: Paul H Brookes Publishing.

Jones, G. (1991). Gender differences in science competitions. *Science Education, 75*(2), 159–167.

Kotte, D. (1992). *Gender differences in science achievement in 10 countries*. Frankfurt: Peter Lang.

National Science Foundation. (2017). *Women, minorities, and persons with disabilities in science and engineering: 2017*. Special Report NSF 17-310. Arlington, VA: National Center for Science and Engineering Statistics. Retrieved from https://www.nsf.gov/statistics/2017/nsf17310/

Olson, L. S. (1985). *The North Dakota Science and Engineering Fair: Its history and a survey of participants*. Unpublished master's thesis, North Dakota State University.

Sackes, M., Trundle, K. C., Bell, R. L., & O'Connell, A. A. (2011). The influence of early science experience in kindergarten on children's immediate and later science achievement: Evidence from the Early Childhood Longitudinal Study. *Journal of Research in Science Teaching, 48*(2), 217–235.

Steinkamp, M. W., & Maehr, M. L. (1983). Affect, ability, and science achievement: A quantitative synthesis of correlational research. *Review of Educational Research, 53*(3), 369–396.

Wolfe, L. (2018, August 30). Statistics on the number of women surgeons in the United States. *The Balance Careers*. Retrieved from https://www.thebalancecareers.com/number-of-women-surgeons-in-the-us-3972900

Worth, K. (2010). Science in early childhood classrooms: Content and process. *Early Childhood Research & Practice, 12*(2), 1–7.

4

GROW THE NUMBER OF WOMEN IN TECHNOLOGY AND ENGINEERING

This chapter will explore the representation of women in technical careers, including jobs in the "T" (technology) and "E" (engineering) STEM fields. While we explored the domains of math and science individually, we will explore these fields together for several reasons. First, in both technology and engineering careers there is a significant gender disparity favoring men. After overcoming barriers to even arrive in these fields, women in technical and engineering domains have similar experiences of isolation, sexism, and pay inequity. The underrepresentation of women in the technical STEM fields is much more drastic than in mathematics and many of the sciences. For these reasons, technology and engineering have been grouped together in this chapter for exploration. Additionally, it is important to keep in mind that many of the tools and curriculum presented later in this book will focus on technology, engineering, and computer science, simply because these are the STEM fields that most need to increase the numbers of girls and women.

TECHNOLOGY AND ENGINEERING OVERVIEW

In many STEM fields, as we saw in the previous chapter, female participation has been on the rise. This has not been the case, however, for careers in technology and engineering fields (National Center for Science and Engineering Statistics, 2013; National Center for Women and Informational Technology, 2011; National Science Foundation, 2017). Fields like computer science are still predominantly male (National Science Foundation, 2017). Women's participation in engineering and computer science on the whole remains below 30%, and women still make up less than 15% of engineers and only 25% of computer and math scientists combined (National Center for Science and Engineering Statistics, 2013; National Science Board, 2014).

The problem is not only *getting* women into the technology and engineering workforce, but *keeping* women there. Women employed in the fields of engineering and computing tend to leave their jobs at higher rates than men do (Corbett & Hill, 2015). One important factor explaining why women are more likely than men to leave engineering (compared to other fields) is dissatisfaction over pay and promotion opportunities (Hunt, 2016).

Moreover, the influence of a male-dominated culture on the tech industry may increase the likelihood that women will have negative professional experiences. High-profile sexual harassment and gender discrimination complaints and lawsuits against tech companies are increasingly being brought into the national spotlight, and highlight ongoing workplace environment problems for women in the technical STEM fields that must be addressed (Benner, 2017).

The problem of female underrepresentation in technology and engineering begins long before women enter the professional world. Recent research has highlighted gender differences in confidence, interest, and performance in technical STEM fields such as engineering, robotics, and computer science beginning in elementary school. This chapter will highlight some of the key gender differences and when they begin to emerge, while parts II and III of this book will cover how parents and educators can begin to address these differences starting in early childhood.

Before we begin, let's review what we mean by "T" (technology) and "E" (engineering) STEM fields. When we talk about technology and engineering, we are talking about exploring our *human-made* environment (as opposed to our *natural* environment). We are thinking about the development and application of tools, machines, materials, and processes to solve the problems humans face every day. Table 4.1 provides examples of some concepts, skills, and jobs from these fields as they may appear in K–12 educational settings (and beyond). You can see a great deal of overlap between technology and engineering, and can certainly see areas where technology and engineering concepts go hand in hand even without explicit curriculum integration. Many of the activities that fall into one category could just as easily fall into the other.

TECHNOLOGY AND ENGINEERING IN EARLY EDUCATION

For a long time, early childhood curriculum has focused on fostering literacy and numeracy skills above all else, with some attention paid to exploring the natural sciences, such as plants, animals, and the environment. When we envision a preschool or kindergarten classroom, we often imagine children practicing their ABCs, counting to 10, and reciting the day's weather. Engineering play, however, has not been totally lost in early childhood settings. Exploring engineering and design through building and exploring with blocks, making bridges out of popsicle sticks, and creating towers with DUPLOs and LEGOs has been (and continues to be) commonplace in most early education settings.

When it comes to technology, we see something slightly different. With the exception of a few computers and tablets, digital technology

Table 4.1.   "T" and "E" Subjects and Fields

Subject	Examples of Relevant Concepts, Jobs, and/or Skills
"T": Technology	Coding/Computer Programming Computational Thinking Sequencing Algorithms Computer Art/Technology-Mediated Design Technology-Mediated Communication Web Design Problem-Solving
"E": Engineering	The Design Process Planning/Blueprinting Sturdy Building Architecture Hardware/Electrical Work Robotics Testing and Improving on Products Problem-Solving

has historically been far less present in early learning environments. Tools like robotics kits and programming languages that have been used with older children for quite some time are only recently being found in early childhood settings. This may be because until recent years, there have been very few commercially available engineering and robotics tools available for very young children. Technology (especially the oft-maligned "screen-based" technology) just didn't *fit in* with the typical image of a preschool or kindergarten classroom. And yet, there is a need to teach technology to young children.

While understanding the natural world is important, developing children's knowledge of the human-engineered and technical world is also an important part of early education today (Bers, 2008). It is important to begin technology and engineering instruction and the development of technological literacy by building on children's natural inclination to design and build things, and to take things apart to see how they work (Resnick, 2007).

Luckily, that doesn't need to mean plopping playful young children in front of screens. Today there are a whole host of technologies designed explicitly for early childhood education—many of which are tangible, playful, and 100% screen-free. We will be exploring some of these tools in part III, along with tips on how to pick effective tools and technologies for girls.

GENDER DIFFERENCES: EARLY CHILDHOOD AND ELEMENTARY SCHOOL

We have already established that there are major gender gaps in the professional "T" and "E" fields—but when do these gaps begin to appear? Gender differences in confidence and interest in these domains begin a lot sooner than you may think. A study that examined how young children (around seven years old) program revealed that gender differences between boys' and girls' performance were related to three main variables: the number of moves made, time taken, and the number of errors made (Yelland, 1993). Moreover, results also found that girls in the study were more careful and less likely to take risks to achieve the task goal than were boys, or boy/girl pairs working together (Yelland, 1993).

In studies on gender and robotics and programming conducted by the DevTech Research Group at Tufts University, several notable gender differences were uncovered at the early childhood level. At the kindergarten level, DevTech's research has shown that boys already perform significantly better than girls on certain advanced programming and building tasks, including properly attaching robotic materials and programming with conditional ("If") statements (Sullivan & Bers, 2013). And in a follow-up study with a sample of children in kindergarten through second grade, similar findings were revealed: while there were no gender differences on *simple* programming tasks, boys performed significantly better than girls on many *advanced* programming tasks such as programming with repeat loops with sensor parameters (Sullivan & Bers, 2016). During the later elementary years, there is some evidence from other researchers that boys may already be more interested in pursuing technical STEM fields than girls. For example, Cunningham & Lachapelle (2010) found that elementary-aged boys were significantly more likely to agree that they would enjoy being an engineer than did girls.

Despite these discouraging findings, research also shows the positive impact that STEM programs, and robotics and coding interventions in particular, can have on increasing girls' interest in engineering during their early childhood and early elementary years (Sullivan, 2016; Sullivan & Bers, 2018a). We have also seen that when specifically choosing developmentally appropriate tools and creating technology and engineering curriculum designed to stimulate the interests of all genders, adults can mitigate gender differences in performance on programming tasks (Sullivan, 2016; Sullivan & Bers, 2018a). This is particularly evident when girls have female robotics teachers (Sullivan & Bers, 2018b). This newer line of research speaks to the importance of early childhood technology interventions and positive female role models in order to engage girls in technical STEM fields.

BEYOND EARLY CHILDHOOD

By high school, male students are more likely than female students to take the standardized exams most closely associated with the fields of engineering and computing (Corbett & Hill, 2015). Female high school students are less likely to decide to take Advanced Placement (AP) computer science classes or express interest in pursuing an undergraduate computer science major (Doerschuk, Liu, & Mann, 2007; Gal-Ezer & Stephenson, 2009; Zweben & Bizrot, 2015).

When it comes to robotics, female students are more likely to have struggled with programming than male students, and female students typically enter a robotics program with less confidence than their male counterparts (Nourbakhsh, Hammer, Crowley, & Wilkinson, 2004). By this time, many female students who may have otherwise been interested in pursuing technology or engineering fields have lost interest, confidence, and the desire to seek out these experiences. Therefore, it is extremely important to make sure these female students have the confidence and skills they need long before they reach high school and college.

LOOKING AHEAD

This chapter has highlighted a major gender disparity between men's and women's representation in technology and engineering fields at the professional level. Beyond that, it has shed light on troubling gender differences in children's confidence and performance on tasks in technology and engineering fields that begin as early as kindergarten, with boys already outperforming girls in such domains as coding. You may be asking yourself: Why do these differences occur? How and why do they begin so early?

The next part of this book will answer those questions as we explore the powerful role of stereotypes, media, advertising, and role-modeling on children's developing ideas about gender and their personal abilities in STEM. We will see how girls' performance on tasks can be drastically influenced by the triggering of stereotypes, and that their performance may not accurately represent their abilities.

This chapter has also hinted briefly at some of the research on eliminating gender differences in technology and engineering performance at the early childhood level and increasing girls' interest in engineering early on. There are many simple actions and practices that adults can take to reduce the impact of these harmful gender stereotypes on young children. We will explore all the ways that parents and educators can make amazing changes in girls' confidence, interest, and abilities in STEM in part III of this book.

REFERENCES

Benner, K. (2017, June 30). Women in tech speak frankly on culture of harassment. *New York Times*. Retrieved from https://www.nytimes.com/2017/06/30/technology/women-entrepreneurs-speak-out-sexual-harassment.html

Bers, M. U. (2008). *Blocks, robots and computers: Learning about technology in early childhood*. New York: Teacher's College Press.

Corbett, C., & Hill, C. (2015). *Solving the equation: The variables for women's success in engineering and computing*. Washington, DC: American Association of University Women.

Cunningham, C. M., & Lachapelle, C. P. (2010). The impact of Engineering is Elementary (EiE) on students' attitudes toward engineering and science. *American Society for Engineering Education*. Retrieved from https://www.eie.org/sites/default/files/research_article/research_file/ac2010full549.pdf

Doerschuk, P., Liu, J., & Mann, J. (2007). Pilot summer camps in computing for middle school girls. *ACM SIGCSE Bulletin, 39*(3), 4. doi:10.1145/1269900.1268789

Gal-Ezer, J., & Stephenson, C. (2009). The current state of computer science in US high schools: A report from two national surveys. *Journal for Computing Teachers, 1*, 1–5.

Hunt, J. (2016). Why do women leave science and engineering? *ILR Review 69*(1), 199–226.

National Center for Science and Engineering Statistics. (2013). *Women, minorities, and persons with disabilities in science and engineering: 2013*. Special Report NSF 13-304. Arlington, VA: National Center for Science and Engineering Statistics. Retrieved from https://ncses.nsf.gov/pubs/nsf19304/prior-releases

National Center for Women and Technology. (2011). *Women and information technology by the numbers*. Fact sheet. Retrieved from https://www.ncwit.org/resources/numbers

National Science Board. (2014). *Science and engineering indicators 2014*. Arlington, VA: National Science Foundation (NSB 14-01).

National Science Foundation. (2017). *Women, minorities, and persons with disabilities in science and engineering: 2017*. Special Report NSF 17-310. Arlington, VA: National Center for Science and Engineering Statistics. Retrieved from https://www.nsf.gov/statistics/2017/nsf17310/

Nourbakhsh, I., Hammer, E., Crowley, K., & Wilkinson, K. (2004). Formal measures of learning in a secondary school mobile robotics contest. Proceedings from ICRA: *IEEE International Conference on Robotics and Automation*. https://doi.org/10.1109/RO-BOT.2004.1308090

Resnick, M. (2007). Sowing the seeds for a more creative society. *Learning & Leading with Technology, 35*(4), 18–22.

Sullivan, A. (2016). Breaking the STEM stereotype: Investigating the use of robotics to change young children's gender stereotypes about technology and engineering. Unpublished doctoral dissertation, Tufts University, Medford, MA.

Sullivan, A., & Bers, M. U. (2013). Gender differences in kindergarteners' robotics and programming achievement. *International Journal of Technology and Design Education, 23*(3), 691–702.

Sullivan, A., & Bers, M. U. (2016). Girls, boys, and bots: Gender differences in young children's performance on robotics and programming tasks. *Journal of Information Technology Education: Innovations in Practice, 15*, 145–165.

Sullivan, A., & Bers, M. U. (2018a). Investigating the use of robotics to increase girls' interest in engineering during early elementary school. *International Journal of Technology and Design Education*. https://doi.org/10.1007/s10798-018-9483-y

Sullivan, A., & Bers, M. U. (2018b). The impact of teacher gender on girls' performance on programming tasks in early elementary school. *Journal of Information Technology Education: Innovations in Practice, 17,* 153–162.

Yelland, N. (1993). Young children learning with LOGO: An analysis of strategies and interactions. *Journal of Educational Computing Research,* 9(4):465–486.

Zweben, S., & Bizrot, B. (2015). 2014 Taulbee survey. *Computer Research News,* 27(5). Retrieved from https://cra.org/wp-content/uploads/2015/06/2014-Taulbee-Survey.pdf

Part II

Stereotypes Are Everywhere (And It's Becoming a Real Issue)

5

WHAT TO KNOW ABOUT GENDER IDENTITY AND STEREOTYPES IN EARLY CHILDHOOD

During free choice time, kindergarteners José and Adriana play in the dress-up area. Adriana puts on a hat and boa. José puts on a plastic pearl necklace and carries a purse on his shoulder. Adriana giggles and says, "José! Boys don't wear jewelry! They don't hold purses!" José replies, "Some boys do." Adriana shakes her head firmly and says, "No, those are for girls only." José shrugs and takes the purse and necklace off and the kids continue playing dress up. Their teacher, Mr. Gardner, observes this from nearby and contemplates how (or if) he should address these gender stereotypes. The classroom is busy, the moment passes, and the comments go unaddressed.

The next day, Mike and Stephanie are working with LEGOs during center time. Mike has assembled a car using a variety of LEGO bricks, axles, and wheels. Stephanie has built a small tower. "How did you make that car, Mike?" she asks him. Mike replies, "I dunno. I just built it." Stephanie looks at it and tries to copy his design, but can't figure out how to attach the wheels to the LEGOs. She gets frustrated and says, "I can't do it!" Mike says, "It's okay, girls aren't as good at building. I'll help you." He takes the pieces out of her hand and builds a second car while Stephanie watches. When he's done he hands it to her. "Thank you!" she says and the two push their cars around the carpet.

Stephanie never learns to build the car on her own, and the comment "girls aren't as good at building" seems to be accepted as fact by both students. Once again, Mr. Gardner isn't sure how he should address the gender stereotype. The two kids had worked together to resolve a dilemma and are now playing happily, so he decides not to intrude.

The comments stick with Mr. Gardner and he decides to observe the comments and actions of his students closely over the next couple of weeks. He hears a range of stereotyped ideas about what girls and boys "should" do. He hears comments about how they should dress, behave, what kinds of activities they are good at, and more. He hears their ideas about what types of jobs moms and dads can and can't have. Mr. Gardner isn't too surprised by some of the common gender stereotypes about appearance (and he knows he needs to address them), but he is surprised to hear many stereotypes about girls' abilities in STEM. He decides to bring this up with his colleagues at their next teacher meeting.

Ms. Daniels shares, "Oh, I hear it all the time too! Especially about math and science. Girls aren't good at math. Girls don't like building things like LEGOs. My dad is the only one that builds things in my house. Things like that. So, I make sure to talk about these ideas during circle time and share some books and pictures of female scientists and engineers. And I tell them I'm a girl who likes LEGOs, so that can't be true of all girls! Sometimes they just need one example to counteract a stereotype they have."

Mr. Gardner is inspired by Ms. Daniel's circle time discussions that directly address her students' stereotypes, and decides to end the week with his own. He tells the students he has been hearing a lot of things about what boys and girls "should" be doing and he wants to talk about them. They make a list on the chalkboard of all their ideas about boys and girls. They talk about why not all of the ideas are true and why they might be harmful or hurtful to say.

Over the next few weeks Mr. Gardner challenges these stereotyped gender notions by reading books that show men and women dressing in a range of clothes and accessories, different types of family and parental arrangements, men and women with a variety of professions, and more. He brings in lab-coats, test tubes, hard hats, and tools to add to the dramatic play dress-up area, encouraging all students to use the clothes and accessories. He reminds them that there are no clothes in the dress up area that are just for boys or just for girls.

Mr. Gardner also works to bring in parent volunteers, including women working in the sciences, men working in caregiving roles (such *as full-time parents), and more to continue counteracting the kids' stereotypes about men's and women's abilities. He even tells the students a story about his own experience with gender stereotypes growing up, saying, "I always knew I wanted to be a kindergarten teacher, but a lot of my friends told me that being a teacher was a girl's job."*

As the months progress, Mr. Gardner becomes more comfortable talking about the kids' gender stereotypes. He sees his students experimenting with their identities and interests more freely. He knows it is normal for his students to have stereotyped ideas of gender as their gender identity continues to develop, and now he feels prepared to address them as they come up. His hope is that his students grow up feeling unencumbered by stereotyped gender expectations and societal pressures.

For over half a century, psychologists and child development researchers have studied how young children develop their ideas about gender and gender identity (Bem, 1981; Bussey & Bandura, 1999; Kohlberg, 1966; Martin & Halverson, 1981; Ruble & Martin, 1998; Trautner, et al., 2005; Zosuls et al., 2009). Gender is something that children are actively working to make sense of and apply meaning to in their own lives. It is also an aspect of development that teachers, parents, and caregivers often struggle with, and are unsure how to discuss with their kids.

Young children use stereotypes to put people, activities, and objects into categories that make sense to them. This is a normal and important part of development—but when do they become harmful? When and how should adults like Mr. Gardner intervene? Should he intervene at all? If you are asking these questions, you are not alone. This chapter introduces common theories on gender development and explores the ways that young children are developing and using gender stereotypes at an early age. It provides initial suggestions for how adults can foster healthy gender development with young children, including providing opportunities for children to act outside of "traditional" gender roles.

THE DEVELOPMENT OF GENDER IDENTITY IN YOUNG CHILDREN

Gender identity refers to one's sense of being male, female, or another gender (American Psychological Association, 2011; 2012). It is important to note that gender identity does not need to be aligned with physical sex assigned at birth. Gender identity is one's own internal perception of the self as male, female, both, or neither.

Gender is no longer seen as a simple binary "he versus she" anymore. Instead, it is far more nuanced and complicated than that. It is beyond the scope of this book to delve too far into this rich and complex topic. Instead, we will focus on the particular experiences and stereotypes of those who identify as female. To understand these experiences, it is necessary to give a brief overview of the way that young children begin to understand the complex world of gender.

During early childhood, between the ages of three and five, children begin to develop their sense of gender identity. They begin to form ideas of what it means to be male or female—or what doesn't fit into either category. For young children, their initial exploration of gender often begins with understanding the sex they are assigned at birth, but it does not stop there. Developing a gender identity is a process that intertwines feelings and experiences with your *physical* body, your *internal feelings* about your identity, and how you *outwardly* express your identity to the world. As we will see in chapter 8, children's ideas about gender are in many ways informed by children's social models, including parents, siblings, peers, and even the media.

There are several major theoretical perspectives on gender identity development, including cognitive development theory (Kohlberg, 1966), gender schema theory (Bem, 1981), and social learning theory of gender development (Bandura, 1977; Mischel, 1966). Each of these theories sheds light on the complex ways in which children develop their sense of gender.

Like many child development theories, Kohlberg's cognitive theories of gender presents a "stage theory" of gender: at each stage of development, children think about gender in an increasingly complex way. Kohlberg suggests that cognition comes before behavior. This means that as children develop cognitively, they in turn mature through their actions. Kohlberg's (1966) stages of gender development are as follows:

1. *Gender identity*: Usually achieved by age two. At this stage children are able to label their own sex.
2. *Gender stability*: Usually achieved by age four. At this stage children realize that gender remains the same over time. Understanding is heavily influenced by external features (for example, a boy in this stage might say things like, "If I wear a dress then I'm a girl").
3. *Gender constancy*: Usually achieved by age seven. At this stage children understand that gender is independent of external features such as haircuts or clothing.

In contrast, social learning theory focuses on the influences of those around us. It suggests that gender identity and gender roles develop through observational learning. According to this perspective, the way that children learn gender behaviors is primarily through a process of *observing* people's behaviors with relation to gender, and later *imitating* the behaviors they learned. One drawback of social learning theory is that it cannot easily explain how children's understanding of gender changes over time. But taken together with cognitive stage theories of gender development, the social learning perspective offers insight into the power of role models and cultural influences on gender development.

The gender schema perspective relates to cognitive theories of gender as well as social learning theories of gender to explain how we become gendered within society. It suggests that once children have developed their gender identity, they search their environment for information that will help them develop their "gender schema."

According to the gender schema perspective, children adjust their behavior to align with the gender norms of their culture beginning in their earliest stages of social development. This perspective was first introduced by Sandra Bem in 1981 and was heavily influenced by the cognitive revolution of the 1960s and 1970s. Bem believed that gender schemas were limiting for men, women, and society as a whole. She believed that raising children beyond the constrictions of these stereotypes and limitations would lead to greater freedom. This perspective is well-aligned with the current push for eradicating gender stereotypes in order to encourage all children to achieve their best selves.

DEVELOPMENT OF GENDER STEREOTYPES

When developing a sense of gender identity, stereotypes can play a major role in how we see ourselves. After becoming gender aware, young children begin to apply stereotypes to themselves and others (Aina & Cameron, 2011; Martin & Ruble, 2004). Stereotypes are defined as a set of beliefs about the characteristics or attributes of a group (Judd & Park, 1993).

All societies have stereotypes, and they help people rapidly process and make sense of the vast differences between us. Stereotypes help young children, who are in the process of understanding sorting based on similarities and differences, make sense of their world and help to create a system of categorizing individuals into groups (Keefe, Marshall, & Robeson, 2003). Stereotypes about a group can be positive (e.g., boys are good at math) or negative (e.g., women are bad drivers).

Gender stereotyping emerges alongside the development of gender identity in early childhood. Basic stereotypes begin to develop in children around two to three years of age (Kuhn, Nash, & Brucken, 1978; Signorella, Bigler, & Liben, 1993). By around 26 months of age, children become most aware of gender differences associated with adults. These differences may include physical appearance or roles (Halim & Ruble, 2010). By 32 months of age, children show awareness of gender stereotypes about children's toys (Ruble & Martin, 1998). And by five years, when most children are entering kindergarten, children begin exhibiting gender-stereotyped knowledge about traits or more abstract attributes of each gender (Powlishta, Sen, Serbin, Poulin-Dubois, & Eichstedt, 2001).

Cognitive theories of gender posit that children are actively trying to make sense of their environment by using gender cues to interpret the information they are taking in (Martin & Ruble, 2004). These theories emphasize developmental changes in a child's understanding of gender that may be aligned with their growing cognitive abilities. As we saw with Kohlberg's theory of gender development, the early childhood years are an important period of gender identity and stereotype development. Stereotypes become fairly well-developed by the kindergarten through second grade years (ages five through seven) when children are developing strict "all or nothing" views about gender. This makes pre-school a critical time period for dealing with gender stereotypes (Aina & Cameron, 2011).

As children grow older, stereotypes about sports, occupations, and adult roles expand further, and their gender associations become more sophisticated (Sinno & Killen, 2009). McKown & Weinstein (2003) found that awareness of others' stereotypes dramatically increases from ages six to ten. Children who were aware of stereotypes and associated themselves with these negative stereotypes performed lower on a diag-nostic test than those who were not associated with the stereotype (McKown & Weinstein, 2003).

WHAT CAN ADULTS DO?

Stereotypes may play an important role in the way that young children are processing and understanding the people and behaviors that they witness, but they can become harmful when left unaddressed by adults. Gender stereotyping has been found to impact children's perceptions from an early age, including influencing what career pathways they believe are suitable for themselves or others of their gender (Adya & Kaiser, 2005). This is not a recent phenomenon. Early research on gender and career inspiration conducted in the 1970s and 1980s found that perceptions of gender norms were a prominent part of how girls chose careers (Gottfredson, 1981; Hawley, 1971). Gottfredson (1981) suggested that by adolescence, one's choices have already been nar-rowed to those that are "gender-appropriate."

Today, gender stereotypes continue to impact children. Most influ-ences in the lives of young children reinforce existing stereotypes that they have (Ramsey, 2004). Therefore it is important for adult educators and caregivers to help *challenge* these stereotypes and offer children different perspectives. If children are exposed to people and content that counter stereotypes, they are more likely to modify their stereo-typed theories and expand their viewpoints (Brill & Pepper, 2008).

It is important to remember that the worst thing you can do is nothing at all. When you hear children making stereotyped comments or see them acting on stereotypes, parents and educators should take the time, as we saw in the vignette of Mr. Gardner and his students, to address these comments through discussions and activities. Part III of this book provides readers with specific actions that parents and educators can take, but to begin with, try putting the following ideas into practice:

- Use books, photographs, and stories that counter traditional gender stereotypes.
- Expose children to role models working in professions that are outside societal gender norms.
- Offer curricular activities or materials that allow children to act outside of traditional gender roles if they choose to (this could be as simple as additional dress-up materials or as extensive as a formal curriculum unit).
- Foster flexible ideas about gender among young children.
- Have an inclusive view of gender yourself and model your beliefs for children.

REFERENCES

Adya, M. & Kaiser, K. (2005). Early determinants of women in the IT workforce: A model of girls' career choices. *Information Technology & People, 18*(3), 230–259.

Aina, O. E., & Cameron, P. A. (2011). Why does gender matter? Counteracting stereotypes with young children. *Dimensions of Early Childhood, 39*(3), 11–20.

American Psychological Association. (2011). Answers to your questions about transgender people, gender identity, and gender expression. Retrieved from https://www.apa.org/topics/lgbt/transgender.pdf

American Psychological Association. (2012). Guidelines for psychological practice with lesbian, gay, and bisexual clients. *American Psychologist, 67*(1), 10–42.

Bandura, A. (1977). *Social learning theory.* Englewood Cliffs, NJ: Prentice-Hall.

Bem, S. L. (1981). Gender schema theory: A cognitive account of sex typing. *Psychological Review, 88*(4), 354.

Brill, S., & Pepper, R. (2008). *The transgender child: A handbook for families and professionals.* San Francisco, CA: Cleis Press.

Bussey, K., & Bandura, A. (1999). Social cognitive theory of gender development and differentiation. *Psychological Review, 106*(4), 676.

Gottfredson, L. S. (1981). Circumspection and compromise: A developmental theory of occupational aspirations. *Journal of Counseling Psychology Monographs, 28*, 545–579.

Halim, M. L., & Ruble, D. (2010). Gender identity and stereotyping in early and middle childhood. In *Handbook of gender research in psychology,* 495–525. Springer, New York, NY.

Hawley, P. (1971). What women think men think: Does it affect their career choice? *Journal of Counseling Psychology, 18*(3), 193–199.

Judd, C. M., & Park, B. (1993). Definition and assessment of accuracy in social stereotypes. *Psychological Review, 100*(1), 109.

Keefe, N., Marshall, N. L., & Robeson, W. W. (2003). Gender equity in early childhood education. *A world of difference*. Washington DC: National Association for the Education of Young Children, 109–113.

Kohlberg, L. (1966). A cognitive-developmental analysis of children's sex-role concepts and attitudes. In E. MacCoby, (Ed.), *The development of sex differences* (pp. 82–178). Stanford, CA: Stanford University Press.

Kuhn, D., Nash, S. C., & Brucken, L. (1978). Sex role concepts of two- and three-year-olds. *Child Development, 49*, 445–51.

Martin, C. L., & Halverson, C. F. (1981). A schematic processing model of sex typing and stereotyping in children. *Child Development, 52*(4), 1119–1134.

Martin, C. L., & Ruble, D. N. (2004). Children's search for gender cues: Cognitive perspectives on gender development. *Current Directions in Psychological Science, 13*, 67–70.

McKown, C., & Weinstein, R. S. (2003). The development and consequences of stereotype-consciousness in middle childhood. *Child Development, 74*(2), 498–515.

Mischel, W. (1966). A social-learning view of sex differences in behavior. In E. E. MacCoby (Ed.), *The development of sex differences* (pp. 56–81). Stanford, CA: Stanford University Press.

Powlishta, K. K., Sen, M. G., Serbin, L. A., Poulin-Dubois, D., & Eichstedt, J. A. (2001). From infancy through middle childhood: The role of cognitive and social factors in becoming gendered. In R. K. Unger (Ed.), *Handbook of the psychology of women and gender* (pp. 116–132). Hoboken, NJ: John Wiley & Sons.

Ramsey, P. G. (2004). *Teaching and learning in a diverse world*. 3rd ed. New York: Teachers College Press.

Ruble, D. N., Martin, C. L., & Berenbaum, S. A. (1998). Gender development. In W. Damon (Series Ed.) & N. Eisenberg (Vol. Ed.), *Handbook of child psychology: Vol. 3. Social, emotional, and personality development* (5th ed., pp. 933–1016). New York: J. Wiley.

Signorella, M. L., Bigler, R. S., & Liben, L. S. (1993). Developmental differences in children's gender schemata about others: A meta-analytic review. *Development Review, 13*(2), 147–183.

Sinno, S. M., & Killen M. (2009). Moms at work and dads at home: Children's evaluations of parental roles. *Applied Developmental Science, 13*(1),16–29.

Trautner, H. M., Ruble, D. N., Cyphers, L., Kirsten, B., Behrendt, R., & Hartmann, P. (2005). Rigidity and flexibility of gender stereotypes in childhood: Developmental or differential? *Infant and Child Development, 14*(4), 365–381. https://doi.org/10.1002/icd.399

Zosuls, K. M., Ruble, D. N., Tamis-LeMonda, C. S., Shrout, P. E., Bornstein, M. H., & Greulich, F. K. (2009). The acquisition of gender labels in infancy: Implications for sex-typed play. *Developmental Psychology, 45*(3), 688–701.

6

ENSURING GIRLS OVERCOME STEREOTYPE THREAT

The problem is that the pressure to disprove a stereotype changes what you are about in a situation. It gives you an additional task. In addition to learning new skills, knowledge, and ways of thinking in a schooling situation, or in addition to trying to perform well in a workplace like the women in the high-tech firms, you are also trying to slay a ghost in the room, the negative stereotype and its allegation about you and your group.

—Claude Steele, *Whistling Vivaldi: And Other Clues to How Stereotypes Affect Us*

A GROWING THREAT

In chapter 5 we explored young children's development of gender stereotypes. We discussed the role that stereotypes have on children's identity formation and some of the harmful outcomes of gender stereotyping. We also reviewed some initial examples of how adults can counteract these stereotypes. The harmful incidences of stereotyping and discrimination discussed in that chapter can lead to a complex social psychological phenomenon known as "stereotype threat."

Stereotype threat refers to anxiety over the perception that one's performance on a task or activity will be seen through the lens of a negative stereotype (Spencer, Steele, & Quinn, 1999; Steele, 1997). When individuals experience stereotype threat, they worry that if they perform poorly on a given task, test, or activity, their performance will affirm the validity of an existing negative stereotype.

In his book, *Whistling Vivaldi: And Other Clues to How Stereotypes Affect Us,* social psychologist Claude Steele describes the battle with stereotypes as "trying to slay a ghost in the room" (Steele, 2011, p. 111). This "ghost" is the negative stereotype that haunts you with its allegation against you and your social group (i.e., your gender, race, or social class). For a fifth-grade girl who is aware of the stereotype that girls aren't good at math, for example, this may result in extra pressure while taking a math test. This extra pressure may negatively influence her performance on the test, regardless of how prepared she is or how much she actually knows.

In fact, high achieving students working in an area they care about may be even more at risk for stereotype threat. While taking her math test, this fifth grader is suddenly multitasking: trying to complete a series of math problems while also (on some level) juggling gender stereotypes about girls and math, while also grappling with the desire to *disprove* these stereotypes. She does not need to *believe* the stereotype is true for it to impact her performance; simply being *aware* of it can be enough to cause this situational predicament. This is how powerful stereotypes are.

THE HISTORY OF STEREOTYPE THREAT

The term "stereotype threat" was first used by two social psychologists, Claude Steele and Joshua Aronson, and their colleagues in the 1990s. Steele and Aronson (1995) conducted several experiments demonstrating that black college students performed worse on standardized tests than white students—only when their race was emphasized. When race was not emphasized, black students performed equal to or better than white students.

These experiments made a shocking revelation in the world of social psychology: performance in academic contexts can be hindered by the awareness that one's behavior might be viewed through the lens of racial or other stereotypes. This phenomenon was coined "stereotype threat" and became one of the most influential lines of social psychology research ever conducted. The findings by Steele and his colleagues focused on understanding the sociocultural impact of stereotypes on people's performance on certain tasks. It illustrated how an immediate situational context can prevent individuals from performing at their true potential.

The basic premise behind stereotype threat is that if you are in a performance-based situation (a test, project at work, job interview, etc.) in which a negative stereotype exists about your group (your gender, race, ethnicity, socioeconomic status, or another characteristic), your anxiety about being judged or nerves about self-fulfilling the stereotype will be distracting and interfere with your performance. Since its introduction to the field of social psychology, hundreds of studies have been conducted examining the impact of stereotype threat. Today, stereotype threat has become one of the most widely explored social psychological topics (Pennington, Heim, Levy, & Larkin, 2016). In addition to the pivotal studies on race and stereotype threat, researchers have examined many topics, including:

- The impact of stereotype threat on girls and women in STEM (e.g., Ambady, Shih, Kim, & Pittinsky, 2001; Spencer et al., 1999; Walsh, Hickey, & Duffy, 1999).
- The impact of stereotype threat on students from low socioeconomic backgrounds compared to students from high socioeconomic backgrounds on intellectual tasks (e.g., Croizet & Claire, 1998; Harrison, Stevens, Monty, & Coakley, 2006).
- The impact of stereotype threat on men compared to women on social sensitivity (Koenig & Eagly, 2005).
- The impact of "diagnosis threat" (i.e., reminding an individual that their prior brain injury may impact their ability to perform on cognitive tasks) on individuals' performance on memory and intelligence tasks as compared to people in neutral test conditions (Suhr & Gunstad, 2002).

WHO IS AFFECTED BY STEREOTYPE THREAT?

Everyone is susceptible to stereotype threat. After all, everyone belongs to at least one group that is characterized by some sort of stereotype. Any salient social identity can impact performance on a task when there is the possibility that a stereotype might be confirmed. However, there are several factors that may make individuals more susceptible. It is important to remember that stereotype threat can impact any individual who is conscious of stereotypes or a stigma ascribed to their social group, whether they believe these stereotypes or not (Brown & Pinel, 2003; Hess, Hinson, & Hodges, 2009). However, those who also *believe* the stereotypes to be true may be especially susceptible (Elizaga & Markman, 2008; Schmader, Johns, & Barquissau, 2004). Individuals with low self-esteem may also be at a higher risk (Rydell & Boucher, 2010).

Several other conditions that commonly occur in academic and professional environments also lead to the occurrence of stereotype threat, such as completing a task relevant to a stereotype about an individual's group, completing a task that is perceived as challenging, and completing tasks in a context that is likely to reinforce the stereotype. In the current professional climate, these conditions happen to be quite prominent in the work experience for women and individuals of any demographic minority (Roberson & Kulik, 2007).

Research has shown that in the workplace, being in a demographic minority invokes stronger perceptions of stereotype threat (Roberson, Deitch, Brief, & Block, 2003). Moreover, "token" minority representation has been found to only makes things worse, by increasing the prominence of negative stereotypes about underrepresented groups and promoting greater stereotyping (Ely, 1995). This leads to a chicken-and-egg problem: we need more diverse representation in workplace environments to lessen the prevalence of stereotype threat, but the presence of stereotype threat (beginning in early school situations and throughout the professional trajectory) leads to fewer women and minorities entering the very workplace environments that need their representation.

STEREOTYPE THREAT AND STEM

STEM fields have gotten quite a bit of attention in stereotype threat research, beginning with early studies on men and women in mathematics. In Claude Steele's (1997) article, "A Threat in the Air: How

Stereotypes Shape Intellectual Identity and Performance," he paints the familiar picture of boys and girls in a math class:

> The teacher is the same; the textbooks are the same; and in better classrooms, these students are treated the same. Is it possible, then, that they could still experience the classroom differently, so differently in fact as to significantly affect their performance and achievement there? (p. 613)

Steele poses an interesting quandary. With all things being equal, do boys and girls still experience the STEM classroom differently? The answer, unfortunately, is often yes.

In fact, there has been significant research showing that stereotype threat may influence the performance of girls and women on STEM-related tasks. For example, Spencer, Steele, & Quinn (1999) found that women performed significantly worse on a math test if they were first shown information indicating that women do not perform as well as men on math tasks (to trigger the negative stereotype). If the negative stereotype was not triggered (i.e., participants were told that there were no gender differences associated with the math test), women and men performed similarly on the test.

Stereotype threat also impacts women's performance in the field of engineering. In a study by Bell, Spencer, Iserman, & Logel (2003), the researchers found that women performed worse than men when engineering exams were viewed as diagnostic of their ability (i.e., a high stereotype threat situation). However, when the test was viewed as non-diagnostic of ability or gender-fair, women performed just as well as men.

Negative stereotype threat can be triggered by explicit statements or through more subtle and implicit messages. For example, a study by Stricker and Ward (2004) for the Educational Testing Service (ETS) found that moving the standard demographic inquiry about test-taker gender (a reminder of gender identity and an explicit trigger of stereotype threat) to the end of the test resulted in significantly higher performance among women who took the AP calculus test.

STEREOTYPE THREAT AND CHILDREN

It's raining, and the students in Mrs. Chang's second grade class are having recess indoors. A big group of kids are having LEGO building competitions on the rug, seeing who can build things the fastest and sturdiest. Lucy excitedly suggests, "Let's have a contest to see who can build the tallest tower!" The kids agree, sharing high fives and smiles. "Who's going to be in the contest?" asks Billy. "We can all try!" says Lucy. "No, we're going to do teams!" says another child. "Yeah, let's do boys versus girls!" several children shout. Lucy reluctantly agrees.

The children split up by gender, with all girls together on one side of the rug and all the boys on the other. Other kids gather around to watch. "Boys versus girls! Boys versus girls!" the kids playfully chant. Lucy hears a girl say, "It isn't fair to do the teams like this, boys are better at building."

The two teams begin working on their towers. After working for a while, the girls' tower falls. The boys declare a victory. "Boys are better builders!" one child shouts. "We already knew that," another child replies. The excitement dies down and the kids move on to other things.

Young children in pre-kindergarten through second grade are not yet taking high-stakes AP calculus tests or the SATs. But they *are* having everyday experiences where they complete tasks, games, and activities that are often impacted by gender stereotypes. There are lots of reasons that the girls' team in Mrs. Chang's class could have lost this competition that have nothing to do with gender stereotypes. It could have been luck. Maybe they were rushing. Maybe the boys' side of the rug had better pieces.

But one thing is notable in this vignette with regard to stereotypes and stereotype threat: The girls were *primed* with a comment that reminded them of their gender (i.e., breaking up into "boys versus girls," a common way for young children to play and compete) and *reminded of a negative stereotype* about their gender (e.g., the comment made that boys are better builders). This creates the perfect storm for stereotype threat to emerge.

Also noteworthy is that the student who commented "it's not fair; boys are better at building" was a girl herself. These are the types of common interactions, statements, and experiences that girls begin to internalize in early elementary school. With everyday reminders of gender and gender stereotypes, there are so many things swimming around in the back of a girl's head when she sits down to take a math test, use a programming app for the first time, or join in a friendly LEGO building competition. As we saw earlier in this chapter, very subtle cues are often enough to have a negative impact on the performance of girls like Lucy on their STEM task at hand.

As is often the case when watching the interactions of very young children, it can be difficult to understand what causes certain outcomes. Certainly, we cannot know for sure from this vignette if Lucy or the other girls on her team experienced stereotype threat during the building competition. So, what does the research say about when stereotype threat begins to impact children's performance on tasks?

Some research has found effects of stereotype threat beginning in early elementary school, even as early as kindergarten (Ambady et al., 2001; Tomasetto, Alparone, & Cadinu, 2011). However, other researchers have found mixed results or no impact at the early elementary level (Muzzatti & Agnoli, 2007; Neuville & Croizet, 2007; Tomasetto, et al., 2011). Further research at the early childhood level is needed to understand when and how stereotype threat impacts young children's performance on tasks in schools and other settings.

The greatest body of research on stereotype threat is focused on people who are adolescents or older. Beyond the research on the impact of stereotype threat on girls' AP exam experiences described in the previous section, stereotype threat continues to impact women's choices through college and into their careers.

In college, female students who report high levels of stereotype threat in male-dominated majors are more likely to consider changing their majors than women in fields not dominated by men (Steele, James, & Barnett, 2002). Since STEM majors tend to be dominated by men, women in STEM-related fields may be more likely to switch trajectories from these fields after experiencing stereotype threat. This further perpetuates the underrepresentation of women in these majors, continuing the cycle.

REDUCING STEREOTYPE THREAT

Whether stereotype threat begins to impact the *performance* of young children or not, we have seen in chapter 5 that gender stereotypes impact the *experiences* and worldviews of children, beginning in early childhood. The vignette on Mrs. Chang's classroom also showed that kids are talking about and experiencing stereotypes in their play and their peer-to-peer conversations. Part III of this book (chapters 9–12) will provide you with ideas for specific tools, curricular approaches, and best practices that will help to combat STEM stereotype threat and provide girls and women with equal opportunities in STEM fields. In the meantime, there are few practical takeaways to consider in order to reduce the prevalence of stereotype threat in general in the environments where you interact with children:

- *Hold all children to high standards, regardless of gender.* The way that parents, teachers, educators, and caregivers talk to children about their expectations makes a huge impact in children's perceptions of their own abilities. In order to reduce stereotype threat, adults should emphasize that they hold *all* children to high standards when it comes to STEM subjects and projects. Remind children that it is okay if they find certain topics or activities challenging. Tell children that they *all* have the capability to succeed and that you will be sure to help them succeed.
- *Teach about brain plasticity.* The implicit message behind negative stereotypes is that a person is inherently less capable simply because of their race, gender, or another characteristic—regardless of the work or effort they put in. Adults can counter this notion by teaching children, even beginning in early elementary school, a simple lesson about neuroplasticity (or the brain's ability to grow new neural connections and strengthen existing ones). You can simplify this concept by telling young children the brain is like a muscle that can get stronger with more hard work and practice. This is also known as fostering a "growth mindset" in children, a concept we will return to in chapter 11 (Dweck, 2002; 2008).
- *Talk about stereotype threat.* Talking directly about the nerves and anxiety around stereotype threat may be one way to reduce its

impact. With older children, you may want to address this around tests or high-stakes homework assignments and projects by saying something like, "Keep in mind that if you are feeling anxious or nervous while taking this test, this could be the result of negative stereotypes and have nothing to do with your actual ability to do well on the test." From there, you can open up a conversation about the impact of stereotype threat to the degree it makes sense based on the age of the child. With younger children, simply beginning to discuss stereotypes as you encounter them (see the following bullet) can be helpful.

- *Don't let stereotypes go unaddressed.* Children are picking up stereotyped messages from their friends, television shows, advertising, at school, and just about everywhere they go. Whenever possible, stop and talk about the stereotypes you encounter. When you let stereotypes go unaddressed, you leave it up to your young child to process and ingrain the information on their own with the limited information they have. Sparking a conversation can be as simple as asking children for their thoughts and providing examples for why the stereotype is not true after all. Even if children brush off your comments or disregard them, it is important to continue the line of communication and model the way you process the stereotypes you encounter each day and how they make you feel.

- *Promote an environment of fairness and belonging.* Above all, adults who work with young children should focus on their own behaviors and biases to ensure they are fostering a fair and equal space for young children to learn, play, and develop. In the classroom, teachers should ensure they don't consistently call on certain students more often for help with particular subjects or activities. Create projects that are designed to help children *learn*, not to measure innate *ability*—and remind children of this! By teaching children about the benefits of diversity and fostering each student's sense of belonging, you will be less likely to create an environment plagued by negative stereotypes.

REFERENCES

Ambady, N., Shih, M., Kim, A., & Pittinsky, T. L. (2001). Stereotype susceptibility in children: Effects of identity activation on quantitative performance. *Psychological Science, 12*(5), 385–390.

Bell, A. E., Spencer, S. J., Iserman, E., & Logel, C. E. (2003). Stereotype threat and women's performance in engineering. *Journal of Engineering Education, 92*(4), 307–312.

Brown, R. P., & Pinel, E. C. (2003). Stigma on my mind: Individual differences in the experience of stereotype threat. *Journal of Experimental Social Psychology, 39*(6), 626–633.

Croizet, J. C., & Claire, T. (1998). Extending the concept of stereotype threat to social class: The intellectual underperformance of students from low socioeconomic backgrounds. *Personality and Social Psychology Bulletin, 24*(6), 588–594.

Dweck, C. (2002). Messages that motivate: How praise molds students' beliefs, motivation, and performance (in surprising ways). In J. Aronson (Ed.), *Improving academic achievement: Impact of psychological factors on education* (pp. 37–60). San Diego, CA: Academic Press.

Dweck, C. (2008). *Mindsets and math/science achievement.* New York: Carnegie Foundation, Institute for Advanced Study.

Elizaga, R. A., & Markman, K. D. (2008). Peers and performance: How in-group and out-group comparisons moderate stereotype threat effects. *Current Psychology, 27*(4), 290–300.

Ely, R. (1995). The power of demography: Women's social constructions of gender identity at work. *Academy of Management Journal, 38*, 589–634.

Harrison, L. A., Stevens, C. M., Monty, A. N., & Coakley, C. A. (2006). The consequences of stereotype threat on the academic performance of white and non-white lower income college students. *Social Psychology of Education, 9*(3), 341–357.

Hess, T. M., Hinson, J. T., & Hodges, E. A. (2009). Moderators of and mechanisms underlying stereotype threat effects on older adults' memory performance. *Experimental aging research, 35*(2), 153–177.

Koenig, A. M., & Eagly, A. H. (2005). Stereotype threat in men on a test of social sensitivity. *Sex Roles, 52*(7–8), 489–496.

Muzzatti, B., & Agnoli, F. (2007). Gender and mathematics: Attitudes and stereotype threat susceptibility in Italian children. *Developmental Psychology, 43*(3), 747–759.

Neuville, E., & Croizet, J. C. (2007). Can salience of gender identity impair math performance among 7–8 years old girls? The moderating role of task difficulty. *European Journal of Psychology of Education, 22*(3), 307–316.

Pennington, C. R., Heim, D., Levy, A. R., & Larkin, D. T. (2016). Twenty years of stereotype threat research: A review of psychological mediators. *PLOS one, 11*(1), e0146487.

Roberson, L., & Kulik, C. T. (2007). Stereotype threat at work. *Academy of Management Perspectives, 21*(2), 24–40.

Roberson, L., Deitch, E., Brief, A. P., & Block, C. J. (2003). Stereotype threat and feedback seeking in the workplace. *Journal of Vocational Behavior, 62*, 176–188.

Rydell, R. J., & Boucher, K. L. (2010). Capitalizing on multiple social identities to prevent stereotype threat: The moderating role of self-esteem. *Personality and Social Psychology Bulletin, 36*(2), 239–250.

Schmader, T., Johns, M., & Barquissau, M. (2004). The costs of accepting gender differences: The role of stereotype endorsement in women's experience in the math domain. *Sex Roles, 50*(11–12), 835–850.

Spencer, S. J., Steele, C. M., & Quinn, D. M. (1999). Stereotype threat and women's math performance. *Journal of Experimental Social Psychology, 35*(1), 4–28.

Steele, C. M. (1997). A threat in the air: How stereotypes shape intellectual identity and performance. *American Psychologist, 52*(6), 613–629.

Steele, C. M. (2011). *Whistling Vivaldi: How stereotypes affect us and what we can do.* New York: W. W. Norton & Company.

Steele, C. M., & Aronson, J. (1995). Stereotype threat and the intellectual test performance of African Americans. *Journal of Personality and Social Psychology, 69*(5), 797–811.

Steele, J., James, J. B., & Barnett, R. C. (2002). Learning in a man's world: Examining the perceptions of undergraduate women in male dominated academic areas. *Psychology of women quarterly, 26*(1), 46–50.

Stricker, L. J., & Ward, W. C. (2004). Stereotype threat, inquiring about test taker's ethnicity and gender, and standardized test performance. *Journal of Applied Social Psychology, 34,* 665–693.

Suhr, J. A., & Gunstad, J. (2002). "Diagnosis threat": The effect of negative expectations on cognitive performance in head injury. *Journal of Clinical and Experimental Neuropsychology, 24*(4), 448–457.

Tomasetto, C., Alparone, F. R., & Cadinu, M. (2011). Girls' math performance under stereotype threat: The moderating role of mothers' gender stereotypes. *Developmental Psychology, 47*(4), 943.

Walsh, M., Hickey, C., & Duffy, J. (1999). Influence of item content and stereotype situation on gender differences in mathematical problem solving. *Sex Roles, 41*(3–4), 219–240.

7

THE BLUE AISLE VERSUS THE PINK AISLE

The Influence of Media, Advertising, and
Toy Companies

A husband and wife are walking through a department store, shopping for a gift for their niece and nephew, seven-year-old fraternal twins. They think that a LEGO set might be a fun and educational gift to give and it would be something the twins can use together. Walking through the LEGO aisles, the couple is shocked by the difference in the marketing of LEGO kits to boys and to girls. They thought they would be able to get one building set the twins could use together, but the way the boxes are designed and presented in the store tells a different story.

On one side, they see pink and purple kits with boxes featuring smiling mini-figure dolls, posing with friends, animals, and flowers. On the other side, they see action-packed kits full of explosions, fires, and vehicles moving at top speed.

The couple is surprised by the gender stereotypes reinforced in these toys. They discuss how the boys' sets don't reinforce any positive social, emotional, or empathy-related experiences, while the girls' sets feature dolls that don't seem to reinforce a nuanced range of female careers or experiences. While all the sets may engage kids in the same building and engineering content, the packaging and marketing of these sets does not sit right with the couple. They are not sure if this is a decision on the part of LEGO or on the part of the store they are in. They continue walking along and decide to look for another gift for their niece and nephew.

We saw in the previous two chapters that stereotypes are a part of our daily lives, and that when they lead to stereotype threat they can have a profoundly negative impact on how we perform on certain tasks. But where do young children learn about these stereotypes? How do they pick them up and ingrain them? This chapter will explore the many ways that the media, advertising, and toys that young children are exposed to perpetuate stereotypes.

Children learn a lot about gender roles, careers, and hobbies through television, the internet, games, and other media sources. Even those young children who receive limited or no screen time at home take their cues from toys, books, or even their parent's magazines. As we can see in the above vignette, even the packaging and marketing of kids' toys and the layout of department stores can reinforce stereotyped views of gender. It is critical for parents and educators to choose toys and media carefully, and be aware of the messages being presented to young children.

TOYS AND A LONG HISTORY OF GENDER STEREOTYPES

From toy tool boxes to pretend kitchens, one of the many things that toys allow young children to do during playtime is to imagine themselves engaging in adult roles and tasks. Along these lines, girls' toys have historically focused on domesticity from around the 1920s to the 1960s, while toys for boys produced during this time focused on preparing them to be future employees working in the industrial economy (Sweet, 2014). An advertisement for an Erector Set from the 1920s exemplifies this:

> Every boy likes to tinker around and try to build things. With an Erector Set he can satisfy this inclination and gain mental development without apparent effort. . . . He will learn the fundamentals of engineering. (quoted in Sweet, 2014)

Meanwhile, advertisements for girls' toys that same year focused on house cleaning and homemaking. This type of toy marketing set the stage early on for regarding STEM-themed toys as being "for boys" and not "for girls."

We can look back and see how toy marketing during those decades was a cultural product of the time. But fast-forward to the 1990s and the 2000s; the toys that young children play with are *still* laden with stereotyped messaging about gender, even if this is sometimes present-ed much more subtly. This is particularly noticeable around gender and STEM themes.

In 1992, Barbie made headlines for all the wrong reasons when Teen Talk Barbie uttered the phrase, "math class is tough!" Organizations including the American Association of University Women (AAUW) and the National Council of Teachers of Mathematics spoke out against the negative messaging in Barbie's phrase, eventually resulting in the doll staying on shelves without the highly contested phrase within her reper-toire (Associated Press, 1992; Sullivan, 1992).

This moment, however, was not unique in Barbie's story. Barbie, a beloved role model for many young children (especially girls), has regu-larly faced backlash for promoting unachievable physical and beauty standards and embodying anti-feminist sentiments. When it comes to STEM, Barbie once again made headlines for the wrong reasons in 2014 when the book *Barbie: I Can Be a Computer Engineer* (originally published in 2010) was discovered by author and Disney screenwriter Pamela Ribon, who wrote about it on her blog. The post went viral after being picked up by Gizmodo (Ribon, 2014).

In the book, Barbie is working on an idea for a game that will teach young children how computers work. However, Barbie is unable to do this on her own: "I'm only creating the design ideas," Barbie says, laughing. "I'll need Steven and Brian's help to turn it into a real game!" (Marenco, 2013). Not only does Barbie rely on two *male* friends to actually program her game, she ends up giving her computer (and Skip-per's computer) a virus before she can even get her ideas to them. Instead of sending a positive message about females in computing, this book sent young girls ages three to seven just the opposite by reiterating stereotypes about women's capabilities when it comes to technology, coding, and engineering.

Gender stereotypes are not only present in toys themselves, but in the way they are sold and organized in stores, as we saw in the vignette that opens this chapter. It is not uncommon to see shelves of blue boxes of LEGOs and building sets with cars, explosions, and other action-packed images on the boxes next to a smaller section of pink and purple LEGOs and building sets featuring pictures of animals and smiling doll-like figures. This type of organization makes clear assumptions about what type of play girls want to participate in and what type of play boys want to participate in.

Recently, retail chain Target took this stereotype one step further by posting signs with the following aisle listings: "Building sets" and "Girls' building sets." In 2015, pictures of these aisle listings went viral on Twitter and many were outraged by this insulting description, which makes a baseline assumption that building sets are for boys. Keep in mind that the sign did not say *boys'* building sets—just "Building sets"—while girls apparently needed a special sign to let them know there were *also* sets for them. This makes several stereotyped assumptions: 1) "Regular" building sets are not used by girls, 2) Girls need "special" sets just for them, and 3) Boys cannot play with these "special" feminine building sets.

These examples are the headline-grabbing stories that have gone viral or received significant media attention in recent years. But it is not hard to imagine that for every story of gender stereotypes in toys that make headlines, there are hundreds more subtle cues of which we are not immediately aware.

Toys are an important part of early childhood. Children learn, social-ize, and build fond memories with their favorite early childhood toys, sets, and games. Therefore, it is important for adults to be aware of the messaging sent by toys, how they are marketed, and what children learn from them. The good news is there are plenty of amazing STEM toys out there to engage all children with the foundational skills they need (see chapter 9 for examples). Here are a few tips for adults to consider:

- *Play with the toys yourself.* Whether purchasing toys for your classroom, as a gift, or for home use with your own children, the best thing adults can do is play with the toy themselves! Teen Talk Barbie, for example, had many prerecorded phrases, only one of which was "math class is tough!" It would be easy for an adult who did not take the time to play with the doll to miss this. Playing with a toy is the best way to decide if it is appropriate for the child or children for which it is intended.

- *Do your research.* Read reviews online, watch YouTube tutorial videos, and do as much research as you can when choosing STEM toys and products for young children. STEM tools such as robotics kits, science sets, and technologies can be pricey and a big investment. You will want to look for products that have been researched and used with children in order to back up any educational claims being made. Tutorial videos will help you determine how complex the product is, how small the parts are, and allow you to decide if it is a good investment for what you want to achieve.
- *Discuss gender stereotypes.* While playing with your children or shopping for toys, talk about gender stereotypes if you notice any. Provide examples to counteract the stereotypes. Do not assume your child didn't notice the stereotyping.
- *Forget gender guidelines.* When shopping for toys, forget any labels that say "boys' toys" or "girls' toys" or anything else. Simply think about the child's developmental level, interests, and the type of learning or play you want to foster. Boys can and should be encouraged to explore dolls and nurturing in their play. Girls can and should be encouraged to explore building and tinkering in their play. All children should be exposed to all of these things that we know are good for them, regardless of the color of the box or the aisle in which the toys are shelved.

TELEVISION AND DIGITAL MEDIA

Children spend a considerable amount of time consuming television, games, and other digital media each day. According to survey data from the Pew Research Center, 90% of school-age children watch TV, movies, or other videos daily, and 79% play games on an electronic device on a typical day (Parker, Horowitz, & Rohal, 2015). Younger children are also part of this digital trend. About eight out of ten parents with children younger than six years of age also say their children have some screen time on a typical day (Parker et al., 2015).

Due to the amount of time children spend consuming digital media, it is probably no surprise that this is a primary way that children are exposed to gender stereotypes and learn about "acceptable" gender roles. Even children who receive limited screen time at home are still exposed when visiting a friend's house or when their peers are discussing television and movies at school.

Children are also exposed to gender stereotypes in the digital games, apps, and websites they explore. The digital media that children consume can have a powerful impact on their identities and future careers, and STEM is no exception. Media are often children's chief source of information. When watching television, children are frequently exposed to characters in stereotypically gendered occupations (Signorielli, 2009). For children who do not know any scientists or engineers in real life, media provide their main examples for what scientists look like (Steinke et al., 2007). Research has demonstrated that girls who are shown television clips featuring stereotypes of women's behavior, such as talking about their outfits, express less interest in STEM careers than girls who are shown no clips or who are shown clips featuring female scientists (Bond, 2016).

For young children, the media presents ideas about how they should dress, behave, interact, and even what they should believe. Preschoolers and kindergarteners are just beginning to develop their ideas of gender and identity and can be greatly influenced by the media they consume. It is important for adults to be aware of what children are watching, and discuss with them the stereotypes that they are undoubtedly encountering. Additionally, it is important for adults to seek out games, apps, movies, and television shows that encourage positive views of females in STEM fields. Here are some tips for adults who are navigating the sea of television and other media for young children:

- *Limit passive screen time.* The American Academy of Pediatrics recommends limited screen time for young children. Parents and caregivers should go one step further and think about how much *passive* versus *active* screen time children are receiving. Passive screen time will include activities such as watching a show or movie, while active screen time might include animating, using an app to make a robot move, or editing digital pictures. Passive screen time is more likely to be *sending* messages to kids (such as stereotyped messages about gender), while active screen time typically allows kids to *create* their own message.

- *Try out media yourself first.* Just like with toys, it is always ideal for adults to watch the show/movie or play the game/app before they put it in front of children. This allows you to know exactly what type of language use, educational value, and gender depictions are present in the media.
- *Watch and discuss shows together.* Coviewing television shows and movies can make screen time more educational and allow an opportunity to discuss gender stereotypes as they arise. Comment positively on characters that defy gender roles or show non-traditional experiences of masculinity or femininity. Discuss negative or restrictive depictions as well.
- *Research, research, research.* In order to find the best shows, movies, or other digital media for young children, read plenty of reviews and ratings online. Common Sense Media (www. commonsensemedia.org) is an excellent resource for parents and teachers. Common Sense Media is an independent nonprofit organization that helps adults choose media (including apps, games, television, and more) for children and adolescents through ratings, reviews, and more.

Positive Media Messaging Example: *Doc McStuffins*

Not all of the media out there for young children sends negative gender messages. The animated Disney series *Doc McStuffins* is a great example of a show for young children that promotes diversity, problem-solving, and non-traditional gender roles. The show, which is intended for a young audience (about preschool age), centers around an African American family and in particular, six-year-old Dottie (or "Doc") who heals her toys and dolls by replacing batteries, sewing them up, and more.

Dottie wants to be a doctor when she grows up and emulates her mother, who is a pediatrician. Dottie's parents take on a reversal of traditional gender roles: her father stays at home as the primary caregiver, while her mother goes to work. Shows like this one counteract traditional stereotypes about gender roles and careers, and provide positive role-modeling to young children of all genders and backgrounds.

ADVERTISING

Young children ages two through seven are exposed to an average of 13,904 television advertisements each year, which represents more than 106 hours a year of advertising (Gantz, Schwartz, Angelini, & Rideout, 2007). This number is even higher for children slightly older. Children ages 8–12 view an average of 30,155 ads, or 230 hours, a year (Gantz et al., 2007).

Advertising is also no longer limited to television or print ads. Children are now receiving messages through a variety of digital media including online advertisements and "advergaming" (games featuring branded content or ads). And although it is illegal in the United States for companies to collect data from children under 13 years of age, there is evidence that indicates that some marketers engage in this practice anyway (Dahl, Eagle, & Báez, 2009).

It is important for adults to be vigilant about the marketing messages children are receiving. Young children are the most vulnerable audience for the messaging portrayed in advertising. Therefore, adults should do whatever they can to limit young children's exposure to advertising by choosing games and apps that do not have pop-up advertisements or in-app purchases.

Television streaming services like Netflix now allow parents to play television shows for young children without any commercial interruption. If kids *are* exposed to ads while watching television through another medium, adults can turn this into an opportunity to positively comment on advertisements that break gender stereotypes. These non-traditional ad campaigns can help to counteract stereotypical beliefs about men and women.

Regardless of how many precautions parents take, children are bound to be exposed to advertisements that do not always have the best messages. This can be a wonderful opportunity to start a dialogue with children about how the ad could be improved. Talk to children about *why* the ad is not the best, and ask their opinions on how they might change it to be better and more inclusive. Prompt children to think about the people they are seeing in the ad, as well as people who might not be represented on-screen.

WHAT DOES AN ENGINEER OR SCIENTIST LOOK LIKE?

For better or worse, digital media, advertising, games, and commercial products influence the way young children view themselves and their abilities. The media can be some children's only exposure to doctors, inventors, engineers, and scientists and, therefore, can shape the vision children have about what these people look like. Studies using the Draw-a-Scientist Test, which prompts participants to draw a picture of a scientist (with no other guidelines), have revealed that drawings more often depict men than women (Rahm & Charbonneau, 1997; Song & Kim, 1999; Thomas, Henley, & Snell, 2006). This illustrates (literally) the common implicit stereotype that people have of scientists. Based on all the images and messages they have seen and consumed, when they are asked to imagine a scientist, they imagine a man. (Many of you may have imagined men when participating in a similar exercise in the introduction to this book!)

It would be easy for adults to condemn all digital media as negative, but this would be a shame. The internet, and online social media in particular, are also powerful places for voices to be heard and stereotypes to be challenged. For example, when sexist comments were posted in response to an ad featuring a female engineer, the #ILookLikeAnEngineer movement was launched. Isis Wegner, the woman featured in the advertisement for her company, was shocked by the backlash her appearance in the ad stirred up and decided to use it as a chance to challenge misconceptions of what a person working in tech "should" look like (Guynn, 2015). She launched the #ILookLikeAnEngineer hashtag on Twitter, and soon after, hundreds of women and people of color joined in, posting pictures of themselves to show the diverse faces of talent in the tech industry.

Movements like these are powerful. Children should be exposed to seeing faces from all backgrounds and genders working in STEM fields. It is the job of parents and educators to make sure they don't grow up imagining that all scientists and engineers look or behave a certain way. Adults serve as role models who can counteract negative messaging in the media children consume. The next chapter will explore the ways that adult and peer role models can impact children's developing ideas about gender, both positively and negatively.

REFERENCES

Associated Press. (1992, October 21). Company news: Mattel says it erred; Teen talk barbie turns silent on math. *New York Times.* Retrieved from https://www.nytimes.com/1992/10/21/business/company-news-mattel-says-it-erred-teen-talk-barbie-turns-silent-on-math.html

Bond, B. (2016). Fairy godmothers > robots: The influence of televised gender stereotypes and counter-stereotypes on girls' perceptions of STEM. *Bulletin of Science, Technology, & Society, 36*(2), 91–97.

Dahl, S., Eagle, L., & Báez, C. (2009). Analyzing advergames: Active diversions or actually deception? An exploratory study of online advergames content. *Young Consumers, 10*(1), 46–59.

Gantz, W., Schwartz, N., Angelini, J. R., & Rideout, V. (2007, March). *Food for thought: Television food advertising to children in the United States.* Kaiser Family Foundation report. Retrieved from https://kaiserfamilyfoundation.files.wordpress.com/2013/01/7618.pdf

Guynn, J. (2015, August 3). #ILookLikeAnEngineer challenges stereotypes. *USA Today.* Retrieved from https://www.usatoday.com/story/tech/2015/08/03/isis-wenger-tech-sexism-stereotypes-ilooklikeanenginer/31088413/

Marenco, S. (2013). *Barbie: I can be a computer engineer.* New York: Random House Children's Books.

Parker, K., Horowitz, J. M., & Rohal, M. (2015, November). *Parenting in America: Outlook, worries, aspirations are strongly linked to financial situation.* Pew Research Center. Retrieved from https://www.pewresearch.org/wp-content/uploads/sites/3/2015/12/2015-12-17_parenting-in-america_FINAL.pdf

Rahm, J., & Charbonneau, P. (1997). Probing stereotypes through students' drawings of scientists. *American Journal of Physics, 65*(8), 774–778.

Ribon, P. (2014, November 18). Books: Barbie f°cks it up again. *Gizmodo.* Retrieved from https://gizmodo.com/barbie-f-cks-it-up-again-1660326671

Signorielli, N. (2009). Race and sex in prime time: A look at occupations and occupational prestige. *Mass Communication and Society, 12*(3), 332–352.

Song, J., & Kim, K. S. (1999). How Korean students see scientists: The images of the scientist. *International Journal of Science Education, 21*(9), 957–977.

Steinke, J., Lapinski, M., Crocker, N., Zietsman-Thomas, A., Williams, Y., Evergreen, S., & Kuchibhotla, S. (2007). Assessing media influences on middle school-aged children's perceptions of women in science using the Draw-A-Scientist Test (DAST). *Science Communication, 29*(1), 35–64.

Sullivan, K. (1992, September 30). Foot in mouth Barbie. *Washington Post.* Retrieved from https://www.washingtonpost.com/archive/politics/1992/09/30/foot-in-mouth-barbie/076dd0eb-996c-48f9-8050-e56ab14951b9/?utm_term=.df0d632b6495

Sweet, E. (2014, December 9). Toys are more divided by gender now than they were 50 years ago. *The Atlantic.* Retrieved from https://www.theatlantic.com/business/archive/2014/12/toys-are-more-divided-by-gender-now-than-they-were-50-years-ago/383556/

Thomas, M. D., Henley, T. B., & Snell, C. M. (2006). The draw a scientist test: A different population and a somewhat different story. *College Student Journal, 40*(1), 140–149.

8

THE IMPORTANT IMPACT OF PARENTS, TEACHERS, AND OTHER ROLE MODELS

Seven-year-old Lydia and her mom are watching a movie on Netflix on their iPad. Suddenly, the video stops playing, and an "error" message comes up. "Mommy, what happened? I want to finish watching!" Lydia says, frustrated. Her mom replies, "I'm not sure . . ." She exits Netflix and then re-opens it. She is still getting an error message every time she tries to play the movie.

"Mommy, what are you doing?" Lydia asks, curious. "I'm trying to figure out what the problem is," her mom replies. "Should we ask Daddy? He's really good at technology," Lydia suggests. She knows her dad plays a lot of video games on the iPad and other devices, and she thinks he might know how to fix the problem faster than her mom. "No," replies Lydia's mom. "We can be good at technology too, just like Daddy. We can problem-solve together! There are lots of things we can try."

Lydia's mom is not sure what the problem is with the iPad. Before Lydia was born, she always went to her husband to fix issues with her phone and computer. But she knows it is important to role-model for her daughter that women are just as capable of figuring out technical issues as men are. She figures this might be a teachable moment, even if it would be faster to go to her husband.

She tries lots of things, and explains her thought process to her daughter as she goes. "I'm going to try turning my iPad on and off, because sometimes that can reset things." When that doesn't work, she has an idea: "I'm going to see if the internet is working." She opens the

Safari app. "What website should we try to visit?" she asks her daugh-ter, trying to include her in the process. "Google?" suggests Lydia. They type in "google.com" and get the message "you are not connected to the internet." "Aha!" exclaims Lydia's mom. "We figured out the problem: the internet isn't working! Now that we know the problem, we just have to fix it." Lydia's mom is genuinely excited that she figured out the problem, and Lydia is caught up in the excitement. Somehow, this de-bugging task has become fun!

Lydia and her mother go downstairs to where their wireless router is located. Lydia has never seen it before, and has a lot of questions about it. Lydia's mom tries to answer as many of them as she can—"I have a hypothesis that if we restart our wireless router, then the internet might work again"—and says they can look up more information about how wireless routers work tomorrow. Lydia doesn't know exactly what her mom means, but she is caught up in the excitement of working on this problem together. They restart the wireless router, wait a little while, and then open up their iPad. Google works, and so does Netflix. "So, the problem was that we weren't connected to the internet; we were right!" Lydia's mom exclaims. They high five, and then snuggle up on the couch to finish their movie.

The next week, Lydia is playing a video game with her dad. Her dad says, "That's strange, I don't think my controller is working." Lydia replies, "Do you want me to try to fix it? I can ask Mommy for help; we're really good at technology."

In the previous chapters we have seen that children, even at the youngest ages, are exposed to stereotyped views of gender everywhere they go. From the toys they play with, to the books they read, to the media and advertising they are exposed to, children are often absorbing harmful ideas about the nature of masculinity and femininity that limit their possibilities later in life. Although there is a wide world of influ-ence beyond the control of parents, educators, and caregivers, there is still a lot that adults can do.

In fact, the role-modeling of adult figures can have a profound im-pact on young children's growing sense of self and understanding of gender. This is especially true when it comes to supporting girls and women pursuing STEM. Research has shown that girls with role mod-els have more positive perceptions of STEM subjects, as well as a stronger belief in themselves and their performance in STEM domains

(Microsoft Reporter, 2018). As girls grow up, female role models have been shown to strengthen young women's attitudes toward mathematics and increase their consideration of STEM fields as career options (Cheryan, Siy, Vichayapai, Drury, & Kim, 2011; Corbett & Hill, 2015). Female role models may also prompt women to persist in challenging engineering majors (Amelink & Creamer, 2010).

This chapter explores the impact of role models and mentors beginning in early childhood. You may be thinking of a STEM role model as a professional computer scientist, doctor, or engineer. You may be wondering what type of role model you can be if you are *not* a scientist or engineer yourself. However, when it comes to young children, parents and educators, regardless of their own expertise, can be amazing STEM role models.

As we saw in the vignette of Lydia and her mom, small everyday interactions can be the best chances for adults to shift a child's viewpoint, arm them with confidence, and dispel stereotypes they may have. Significant attention in this chapter will be paid to adult role models, but we will also look at the importance of peer and sibling role models as well.

A role model can be anyone a child looks up to, observes, or admires. Role models can be characters in books, television shows, or stories. They can be grandparents or friends. Therefore, it is important to understand *who* children look up to, and what message these role models are sending. If you are reading this book, you are likely a role model to at least one child. The messages you send with your behaviors and words (especially things you don't think twice about!) will be extremely important to consider as well.

PARENTS

Parents and primary caregivers are the first role models that children encounter. Children look up to their primary caregivers and often go through a phase of desiring to be just like them when they grow up. It is important to think about how parents and caregivers shape children's perceptions of gender roles.

Beginning at birth, parents provide children with their first introduction to gender. From the way they decorate a new baby's nursery, to the clothes, books, and toys they provide, each choice is laden with meaning and reflects parental ideas about gender roles and expectations for the baby. Often, parental choices have the power to either perpetuate or dispel gender stereotypes. Different types of family structures can also influence children's notions of gender in different ways. For example, some research has found that the children of same-gender parents were less gender stereotyped in their play behavior than the children of heterosexual parents (Goldberg, Kashy, & Smith, 2012).

As children grow up, they continue to learn about gender roles from observing their parents and other primary caregivers. For example, whether you realize it or not, young children are actively observing the following:

- *Who does each home-related task (or how these tasks are shared).* This includes activities such as cooking, cleaning, playing with and caring for children, fixing things around the house, and managing finances. How do children in the household share and participate in household tasks? How are they rewarded for their participation in these tasks? A *New York Times* article pointed out that not only do girls tend to do more household chores than boys, they are also paid less for completing chores, on average, than boys (Miller, 2018).
- *What each parent does outside the home.* This includes activities such as going to work, participating in hobbies or sports leagues, going on trips, taking children to school, and participating in children's extracurricular activities.
- *How the parents present themselves.* This includes clothes, jewelry, shoes, and makeup, but it also includes the way parents talk about and describe themselves, including what they are good at, what they are confident in, and how they describe their careers and their role in the family.

When it comes to STEM, parents can also be powerful influencers. Having a parent or guardian who works in a STEM profession makes it more likely for girls to perform well in math and to enroll in STEM degree programs such as engineering, architecture, math, and computer science in college (Sherburne, 2017). However, even parents who are not in STEM fields professionally can be STEM role models.

The role-modeling by parents and parental expectations about girls' abilities and interests can influence how girls see themselves with regard to computers and computing (Margolis & Fisher, 2002). The American Association of University Women (AAUW) agrees, stating that parents should begin sharing information about women in engineering fields as early as possible: "Parents also play an important role in exposing their children both to the fields of engineering and computing generally and to women in these fields at early ages, when their implicit biases are forming" (Corbett & Hill, 2015, p. 108). Parents should consider doing the following with their young children at home to address this recommendation:

- *Provide hands-on STEM play for children.* Parents can foster a love of STEM exploration at home by providing STEM toys to play with, especially engineering and computing toys (part III of this book will provide some suggestions). DIY home science experiments are also a great way to provide kids with hands-on STEM fun. For parents of young girls, be sure to encourage them to explore STEM toys and activities with the same frequency you suggest "traditional" toys like dolls.
- *Perform hands-on STEM by parents.* The best way parents can role-model positive attitudes toward STEM is to show how they use STEM themselves! Talk about math while cooking, measurement while decorating a room, science while gardening, and technology while using your GPS. Make sure you never joke about technology working "by magic." Instead, talk about how engineers developed the technology you use each day and engage your child in a discussion on guessing what's inside your remote control or laptop that makes it work the way it does. (If you have an old computer or a remote, you can do a "technology dissection," letting your child open it up to see what's inside!) Female parents should be especially aware of modeling that they are capable of building and assembling things like furniture, troubleshooting when technology fails, and fixing items that break. Does this mean mom needs to suddenly build and fix everything around the house if she doesn't typically? Not at all. Just be aware that children see what you do and what you don't do. If you are a female parent who does not typically engage in tasks that involve building, tin-

kering, or troubleshooting, consider putting some of these jobs
into your rotation to role-model your capability in these areas,
even if you don't perform these every time.
- *Talk about females in STEM.* Parents should regularly talk about
  female scientists, engineers, doctors, and astronauts with their
  children (if you don't know any, take this time to look some up!
  Table 8.1 provides some starting suggestions). Talk to young children about the different types of STEM jobs out there, from
  zoologists to mathematics professors; there may be many jobs
  they haven't even heard of (a list of examples can be found in
  appendix B). If you know a female working in a STEM field, be
  sure to introduce her to your children. Have her talk about what
  she does and how she uses math and science each day. When
  females in STEM are in the news, be sure to discuss these current
  events with children.

Parents and caregivers should think about how their own behaviors and
beliefs will impact their children. If parents hold gender stereotypes
about fields like math being more important for male children than
female children, for example, this can have a profound impact on girls
and can reduce their daughters' interest in math (Davis-Kean, 2007).
Young children are sponges, so modeling positive attitudes toward

Table 8.1.   Female STEM Role Models You Should Know

Who	What She Did
Marie Curie (1867–1934)	Physicist and chemist Marie Curie pioneered research in the area of radioactivity. Along with her husband, she was the recipient of a Nobel Prize in 1903.
Grace Hopper (1906–1992)	Sometimes called the "Queen of Code," Grace Hopper was a military leader, mathematician, and pioneering computer programmer. She helped work on the Mark I, one of the world's earliest computers.
Jane Goodall (1934–present)	An anthropologist and primatologist, Jane Goodall is one of the most famous primate scientists of all time. She is best known for her work with chimpanzees and as a passionate advocate for animal rights.
Mae Jemison (1956–present)	An astronaut and physician, Mae Jemison was the first African American woman admitted into NASA's astronaut training program. In 1992 she became the first African American woman to go to space.

STEM subjects, and females in STEM, is incredibly important. This means parents must take stock of their own actions and words.

Even when adults do not explicitly say things like "boys are better at building" or "girls aren't good at math," everyday phrases and behaviors can relay this same message. Table 8.2 describes a few common phrases adults tend to say, and why they may be harmful for young children to hear. Once parents have eliminated these no-go phrases, they will be well on their way to modeling positive STEM attitudes and behaviors.

TEACHERS

Teachers are some of the adults that children and adolescents spend the most time with outside the home. Therefore, it is no surprise that teachers can be powerful role models. When it comes to STEM, having female teachers can be especially important. In a study of students enrolled in a calculus class, results demonstrated that both female and male students participated more and asked more questions if the class was taught by a female rather than male professor (Stout, Dasgupta, Hunsinger, & McManus, 2011). For female students, having a female rather than male professor also increased implicit liking of math, and the females identified more with math and their professor (Stout et al., 2011).

Even at the early childhood and early elementary school level, there is preliminary research suggesting the importance of female STEM teachers. These teachers, whether they are teaching robotics, coding, engineering, science, or math, are modeling women's confidence and capability in STEM domains for young children. Research conducted by the DevTech Research Group at Tufts University has demonstrated that when girls in kindergarten through second grade had a female robotics and programming instructor, they performed just as well as male students on all programming tasks assessed. However, when they had a male instructor, boys performed significantly better than girls on advanced programming tasks, especially those that had explicit math connections (Sullivan & Bers, 2018). Why could this have happened? It may have been that just the presence of a male expert in coding and engineering triggered an experience of stereotype threat for the girls, reinforcing beliefs that girls are not as capable in these fields.

Table 8.2.   Common Phrases Parents Should Rethink

Phrase to Avoid	Why?	Say and Do Instead
"I'm just not a math person."	This phrase is a big no-no! It falsely indicates that some people are just "math people" and others aren't. It does not support a growth mindset. If you are a female parent, it further supports stereotypes that women are not good at math.	**Say:** "Hmm . . . this is tricky, but let's see if I can figure it out. It's okay if I make mistakes along the way, right?" **Do**: Actively try to figure out the problem you were trying to solve. Share your thought process aloud while you figure it out, including any mistakes you make. It's okay if you need to get help!
"That's a Daddy activity" or "That's a Mommy activity"	Whatever you are referring to, from playing with LEGOs, to practicing ballet, baking cookies, or working on math homework, making something only a "Mommy" or "Daddy" activity reinforces gender stereotypes about which activities are meant to be done by males or females.	**Say:** "I'm going to do this with you today instead of Daddy—isn't that exciting?" **Do**: It's great to have special time with one parent—but consider switching up the normal parenting routines and activities! If one parent is usually the one who plays sports with the kids, for example, let the other jump in! Be especially aware of this when it comes to STEM routines, such as helping with math homework, doing science experiments, and playing with LEGOs.
"I give up" or "I don't even want to try to figure that out"	A big part of STEM is persistence through challenges and staying goal-focused. Giving up when the going gets tough (or not even trying to begin with) does not model a positive, self-motivated, problem-solving approach.	**Say:** "This is really, really, hard! Part of me wants to stop trying but I know I will feel SO good when I figure this out!" **Do**: Keep trying to solve the problem or issue you were working on! Narrate your problem-solving process out loud. Remember, it is fine to take breaks and return to the problem later.

Whatever the reason, female teachers in STEM fields are certainly important for young children to see. They serve as examples and role models of female experts in STEM, and allow young children to learn skills and content from them. Therefore, it is important for schools to consider the following:

- *Expose children to female STEM "teachers."* This is especially important when it comes to computer science and engineering. These teachers can be specialist teachers, parents, friends who come to teach a guest lesson, or even female high school or middle school students who want to teach a lesson about engineering or coding to younger children! If your school does not have any coding or engineering initiatives in place, consider partnering with a local university and specifically look for female college students who may want to come teach a lesson.

- *Regular classroom teachers should integrate technology and engineering across curricular content.* While specialists and guest engineers can be wonderful role models, regular classroom teachers cannot rely on them alone to be in charge of encouraging and modeling positive STEM attitudes. This is especially true of regular classroom teachers who are female. We have seen in the first part of this book that technology and engineering is generally less present at the early childhood level than science and math, and we have also seen that technology and engineering are domains in which men most drastically outnumber women. Early childhood teachers must begin to address this inequity by integrating subjects like coding, robotics, design, and engineering at the early childhood level. Female teachers in particular should model that they can teach and integrate these subjects and become masters of these domains along with the kids, even if they do not have a formal background in STEM. Chapter 10 will provide examples of activities and curriculum units that teachers can try out.

- *Teach about females in STEM:* Beginning in kindergarten (or earlier), teachers should start talking about female scientists and engineers in school. Teachers can read picture books featuring fictional females exploring STEM (see appendix D for suggestions). Teachers should also follow all of the same advice that was provided to parents in the previous section in order to avoid phrases and behaviors that unknowingly have a negative impact on girls' confidence and desire to pursue STEM.

PEER INFLUENCERS

While adult caretakers, family, and teachers are examples for social modeling, friends and peers are among the biggest influences in the lives of children. From the earliest playdates and interactions children have with one another, they are learning a great deal from their peers. When children interact with peers in preschool and early elementary school, in playgroups and extracurricular settings, they get the chance to practice skills shown to them by adults, such as reading, and counting. However, more importantly, they begin to see school and extracurricular activities as a chance to have fun, be with friends, and meet new children their age.

It is important to begin providing young girls with chances to associate STEM learning with having fun and playing with peers, especially other girls. This can happen through a girls' coding club, a robotics camp, a STEM playgroup, or something similar. Starting a local "Mommy & Me" STEM group in your neighborhood can also be a powerful way for young children to have positive experiences viewing their female caregivers as STEM role models while also allowing girls to interact with peers (children of all genders) who are exploring STEM in a casual, noncompetitive context.

Positive peer influences become increasingly more important as girls grow up; therefore, it is important not to wait until middle or high school to ensure girls have peers who role-model positive STEM attitudes and support STEM pursuits. Research suggests that students' academic achievement and goals can be shaped by their peers. When it comes to STEM, studies have shown that there is a link between peer influences and girls' and women's interest, achievement, and retention in STEM subjects and careers (Herzig, 2002; Margolis, Fisher, & Miller, 2000; Riegle-Crumb, Farkas, & Muller, 2006; Robnett & Leaper, 2013; Stake & Nickens, 2005; Zeldin & Pajares, 2000).

In high school, having close friends who are high-achieving students is associated with a greater likelihood of enrolling in advanced courses, and this is especially true of girls taking advanced math and science courses (Crosnoe, Riegle-Crumb, Field, Frank, & Muller, 2008; Riegle-Crumb et al., 2006). In a nutshell—girls need to be around other girls who enjoy and appreciate STEM. While there is little that adults can do to control with whom their adolescents spend time, at the early childhood level parents and caregivers can provide girls with opportunities to be around other girls who are engaging with STEM content in fun and playful ways. This will set them up for success later on.

Example: STEM and the Girl Scouts

Where can parents go to find positive extracurricular programs for young girls to receive adult mentorship in STEM as well as positive peer interactions? Many traditional programs for girls are now integrating STEM activities into their offerings. For example, recent STEM initiatives by the Girl Scouts of the USA demonstrate how an organization that focuses on female bonding and mentorship can increase girl's interest in STEM.

The Girl Scouts offers programs for girls beginning in kindergarten all the way through high school. Over 160,000 Girl Scouts participate in STEM programs annually (Girl Scout Research Institute, 2016). The content of these programs varies, but they generally focus on increasing girls' interest in STEM, increasing girls' confidence in their STEM-related abilities, educating girls about STEM careers, and exposing girls to STEM professionals (Girl Scout Research Institute, 2016).

Research conducted by the Girl Scout Research Institute (GSRI) has demonstrated the power of girls learning with their female peers as well as from STEM role-models. Girls who completed various Girl Scouts STEM programs say that after participating, they now know that math and science can be fun. The girls also have more positive views of STEM subjects and were more confident as well (Girl Scout Research Institute, 2016).

Participating in programs such as the Girl Scouts checks off a lot of boxes when it comes to providing girls with STEM resources. First off, there is exploration of specific STEM skills and content. But maybe more importantly, it allows girls to be among other girls, their peers, in a fun and social context that dispels many stereotypes about STEM (e.g., that people in STEM work alone or are "nerdy"). In addition to peers, these programs also allows girls to learn from female adults, including parents, volunteers, and in some of the STEM programs, professionals in the STEM career world. With all of these positive female influences, it is not hard to imagine masculine stereotypes about

STEM dissipating—or never forming to begin with—depending on how early girls get involved.

OTHER STEM ROLE MODELS

Thus far we have concentrated predominantly on girls' immediate spheres of influence at home and at school: parents, teachers, and peers. But there are other types of role models that can be positive influences as well. These include the following:

- *Fictional characters:* Fictional characters in movies, books, games, and television shows can have a powerful impact on young children. Consider choosing books and media that showcase girls and women in STEM in a positive light, which provides another outlet for girls to be exposed to female STEM role models. The website Common Sense Media, described in the previous chapter, can be a useful reference to learn more about currently available children's media (see www.commonsensemedia.org). You can also find a list of picture book suggestions that feature females characters exploring STEM in appendix D of this book.
- *Siblings:* Older siblings play an important role in teaching and socializing their younger siblings. Just as parents and caregivers need to take stock of their own behaviors and beliefs to ensure they are modeling positive messages, parents should also take stock of the messages and behaviors portrayed by older siblings. Parents with children of different genders should also ensure that they treat all their children equally and do not have different expectations based on gender, especially when it comes to STEM.
- *Older students:* Young children look up to and admire the older students at their school and in their communities. Older students can be positive role models when it comes to a variety of matters, including STEM. Early childhood teachers can consider a "big buddy" system, pairing their students with those from older grades at their school to complete an engineering or coding project, read an engineering-focused picture book, or complete a science experiment together.

- *Female STEM professionals:* Introducing girls to women who are successfully working in STEM careers, particularly the technical STEM fields, is a very important way to dispel stereotypes about the fields and show girls the possibilities they can aspire to. Teachers can consider partnering with local businesses to bring female scientists and engineers in as guest speakers, or to bring their students to these businesses for a field trip. Local universities, museums, and research labs that focus on science and technology are also a great place for teachers and principals to begin trying to forge partnerships.

ROLE MODELS AND BEYOND

There are clearly many benefits to ensuring that young girls have positive role models in the forms of teachers, professionals, parents, and peers who inspire them to pursue STEM. These role models can also be a powerful buffer against the harmful impacts of stereotype threat. Researchers have found that exposure to female peers and adult role models whose accomplishments in STEM fields contradicts larger societal stereotypes about women in STEM can increase young women's own sense of identification with STEM fields (Dasgupta & Asgari, 2004; Lenton, Bruder, & Sedikides, 2009; Stout et al., 2011). Programs at school, activities and playdates run by parents, and large organizations like the Girl Scouts can all provide young girls with access to STEM content as well as positive STEM role models.

While many initiatives focus on providing girls specifically with female role models for all the reasons previously explored in this chapter, some researchers have found that role model gender is less important than combating current stereotypes of people in STEM fields (Cheryan, Meltzoff, & Kim, 2011). This means role models of *any* gender can be positive influences if they combat stereotypes. In fact, male parental figures may have an even greater influence than female parents in some cases. New research from Microsoft states that "in some areas like computer science, dads can have a greater influence on their daughters than moms, yet are less likely than mothers to talk to their daughters about STEM" (Choney, 2018). This means it is just as important for male teachers, parents, and caregivers to become aware of stereotype threat and the need to engage girls in STEM.

Knowing you need to make changes is only one part of the equation. Actually *doing* something is the other. This part of the book has focused on making you aware of stereotypes and stereotype threat, and its harmful impact on young children. But for adults to really feel prepared and confident in their abilities to be a STEM role model, they need to know how to choose appropriate STEM tools and products and how to develop curricula and activities that will interest girls. Part III focuses on providing advice for adults who wish to reach young girls with fun and engaging STEM content.

REFERENCES

Amelink, C. T., & Creamer, E. G. (2010). Gender differences in elements of the undergraduate experience that influence satisfaction with the engineering major and the intent to pursue engineering as a career. *Journal of Engineering Education, 99*(1), 81–92.

Cheryan, S., Meltzoff, A. N., & Kim, S. (2011). Classrooms matter: The design of virtual classrooms influences gender disparities in computer science classes. *Computers & Education, 57*(2), 1825–1835.

Cheryan, S., Siy, J. O., Vichayapai, M., Drury, B. J., & Kim, S. (2011). Do female and male role models who embody STEM stereotypes hinder women's anticipated success in STEM? *Social Psychological and Personality Science, 2*(6), 656–664.

Choney, S. (2018, March 13). Why do girls lose interest in STEM? New research has some answers—and what we can do about it. Microsoft: Features. Retrieved from https://news.microsoft.com/features/why-do-girls-lose-interest-in-stem-new-research-has-some-answers-and-what-we-can-do-about-it/

Corbett, C., & Hill, C. (2015). *Solving the equation: The variables for women's success in engineering and computing*. Washington, DC: American Association of University Women.

Crosnoe, R., Riegle-Crumb, C., Field, S., Frank, K., & Muller, C. (2008). Peer group contexts of girls' and boys' academic experiences. *Child Development, 79*(1), 139–155.

Dasgupta, N., & Asgari, S. (2004). Seeing is believing: Exposure to counterstereotypic women leaders and its effect on the malleability of automatic gender stereotyping. *Journal of Experimental Social Psychology, 40*(5), 642–658.

Davis-Kean, P. (2007, May 21). Educating a STEM workforce: New strategies for U-M and the State of Michigan. Paper presented at Educating a STEM Workforce Summit, Ann Arbor, Michigan. Retrieved from http://www.ns.umich.edu/htdocs/releases/print.php?htdocs/releases/plainstory.php?id=5895&html

Girl Scout Research Institute. (2016). *How Girl Scout STEM programs benefit girls: A compilation of findings from the Girl Scout Research Institute*. Retrieved from https://www.girlscouts.org/content/dam/girlscouts-gsusa/forms-and-documents/about-girl-scouts/research/How_Girl_Scout_STEM_Programs_Benefit_Girls_GSRI_2016.pdf

Goldberg, A. E., Kashy, D. A., & Smith, J. Z. (2012). Gender-typed play behavior in early childhood: Adopted children with lesbian, gay, and heterosexual parents. *Sex Roles, 67*(9–10), 503–515.

Herzig, A. H. (2002). Where have all the students gone? Participation of doctoral students in authentic mathematical activity as a necessary condition for persistence toward the Ph.D. *Educational Studies in Mathematics, 50*(2), 177–212.

Lenton, A. P., Bruder, M., & Sedikides, C. (2009). A meta-analysis on the malleability of automatic gender stereotypes. *Psychology of Women Quarterly, 33*(2), 183–196.

Margolis, J., & Fisher, A. (2002). *Unlocking the clubhouse: Women in computing.* Cambridge, MA: MIT Press.

Margolis, J., Fisher, A., & Miller, F. (2000). The anatomy of interest: Women in undergraduate computer science. *Women's Studies Quarterly, 28*(1–2), 104–127.

Microsoft Reporter (2018, April 25). Girls in STEM: The importance of role models. Microsoft News Centre Europe. Retrieved from https://news.microsoft.com/europe/features/girls-in-stem-the-importance-of-role-models/

Miller, C. (2018, August 8). A "generationally perpetuated" pattern: Daughters do more chores. *New York Times.* Retrieved from https://www.nytimes.com/2018/08/08/upshot/chores-girls-research-social-science.html

Riegle-Crumb, C., Farkas, G., & Muller, C. (2006). The role of gender and friendship in advanced course taking. *Sociology of Education, 79*(3), 1017–1045.

Robnett, R. D., & Leaper, C. (2013). Friendship groups, personal motivation, and gender in relation to high school students' STEM career interest. *Journal of Research on Adolescence, 23*(4), 652–664.

Sherburne, M. (2017, December 20). A "STEM" parent boosts girls' participation in science degrees. *University of Michigan News.* Retrieved from https://news.umich.edu/a-stem-parent-boosts-girls-participation-in-science-degrees/

Stake, J. E., & Nickens, S. D. (2005). Adolescent girls' and boys' science peer relationships and perceptions of the possible self as scientist. *Sex Roles, 52*(1–2), 1–11.

Stout, J. G., Dasgupta N., Hunsinger M., McManus M. A. (2011). STEMing the tide: Using ingroup experts to inoculate women's self-concept in science, technology, engineering, and mathematics (STEM). *Journal of Personal and Social Psychology, 100*(2), 255–270.

Sullivan, A., & Bers, M. U. (2018). The impact of teacher gender on girls' performance on programming tasks in early elementary school. *Journal of Information Technology Education: Innovations in Practice, 17*, 153–162.

Zeldin, A. L., & Pajares, F. (2000). Against the odds: Self-efficacy beliefs of women in mathematical, scientific, and technological careers. *American Educational Research Journal, 37*(1), 215–246.

Part III

Break the STEM Stereotype in Early Childhood

9

TOOLS, GAMES, AND PRODUCTS TO ENGAGE GIRLS IN PRE-K THROUGH EARLY ELEMENTARY SCHOOL

Eliza walks down the toy aisle with her six-year old daughter, Kelly. Kelly jumps along excitedly, petting all the stuffed animals that she can reach as they walk through a long corridor of purple and pink toys. Kelly stops to pick up a toy cat, grabbing it off the shelf and hugging it. "I want this kitty," Kelly tells her mom. "Come on honey, you have plenty of stuffed animals at home," Eliza says to Kelly, urging her along.

Eliza wants to find Kelly toys she can use to practice the STEM skills she is learning at school. Eliza was really excited to find out at a recent open house that Kelly's teacher has been teaching the class about the engineering design process and coding. Inspired by this, Eliza is looking for toys that will allow her daughter to build, engineer, and problem-solve at home. She never had toys like that growing up and remembers that only her brother was encouraged to use LEGOs and engineering products. She wants Kelly to have a more well-rounded play experience.

"Why aren't there any STEM toys in the girl's toy section of this store?" Eliza wonders. Her son, eight-year-old Sam, has plenty of toys and kits that encourage him to tinker, build, follow blueprints, and create. She wants to find materials that encourage her daughter to practice these same skills.

Eventually, Eliza and Kelly leave the pink-and-purple section and come to the blue section, filled with Star Wars LEGO sets, model airplanes, remote-controlled cars, and sports-themed toys. These look like the kind of toys that fill Sam's bedroom at home. Eliza is struck by how clearly the store has marketed a "boys section" and a "girls section," and she wonders to herself why there can't just be toys for all children, regardless of gender. Eliza sees some toys in the blue section she thinks might be good for Kelly, but wonders how she'll sell her daughter on toys with a boy's face on the packaging. "Do you want one of these, Kelly? They look really fun to build!" Eliza asks her daughter as they pass the model airplane kits. "No, Mommy, I don't like those."

They move past the blue aisles and into another aisle of LEGO kits and construction products. Eliza is pleasantly surprised that this aisle appears to be somewhat gender-neutral, despite the many blue and gray colored LEGO boxes. Here Eliza sees a few STEM products and robotics kits that look promising, but she isn't sure how to choose one. She is also thrown off by how expensive many of the materials are, especially the robots.

As she is reading the back of a box, Eliza sees that Kelly has found some toys in this aisle that interest her. "Look, Mommy! Girl LEGOs!" Kelly says happily. She has found a corner of the LEGO shelf stocked with the LEGO Friends line. "Can I have one of these?" she asks her mom, holding up a pink and purple box. Eliza is happy that her daughter has found something that involves building and creating, but then remembers the yellow tub of primary colored LEGOs and DUPLOs sitting in Kelly's playroom that she rarely uses. "Kelly, you already have LEGOs at home. Do you want to pick something different?" she asks. "These are different, Mommy. They are really different!" Kelly argues. Eliza shrugs and decides to give it a shot.

When they get home, Kelly is excited to open the box. This kit is called "Emma's Deluxe Bedroom" and includes everything you need to build a fun bedroom for a mini doll figure named Emma. Kelly dumps the parts out and begins building the bedroom, complete with a bed, drawing board, pottery stand, and a special stand for her cat to pose on. She meticulously follows the directions, asking for help from her mom when needed. Once everything is built, Kelly pulls out the mini doll figure (Emma) and a cat figure (Chico). She also brings out a few of her other small non-LEGO dolls and plays with all of them in the LEGO bedroom that she built. "Look Mommy, I built them a new dollhouse!" Kelly says happily.

Eliza is amazed. She has never seen her daughter take an interest in LEGOs or building before. However, she also has mixed feelings. Does this mean she will have to exclusively buy "special" LEGOs for her daughter if she wants her to practice tinkering and building? What was wrong with the gender-neutral LEGOs already sitting in the playroom?

Eliza considers the fact that maybe Kelly was excited to build the Deluxe Bedroom because she wanted a new way to play with her dolls and engage in imaginative storytelling. This box provided her with the encouragement she needed to connect building with doll play. Eliza does some research online and discovers that there are a variety of dollhouse-making kits available online, some that integrate motors, lights, and sensors. She decides to take a leap into Kelly's current interest in dolls and integrate engineering into the play she already loves.

Over the next few days, she encourages Kelly to use her other LEGOs as well as recycled materials found around the house to continue expanding on the dollhouse she created. They review the steps of the Engineering Design Process (sent home in a flyer from Kelly's teacher) as they test the new house additions to ensure they are sturdy.

The next week, Eliza surprises her daughter with a new way to expand the dollhouse using a kit called Roominate that she found online. They use batteries, lights, and motors to create an interactive dollhouse that has a spinning fan and a light that turns on. As Eliza and Kelly are working, Kelly's older brother Sam comes over to observe. "Can I help too?" he asks. Eliza beams as she watches Kelly and Sam work together tinkering and building with the new materials.

THE BATTLE OF THE PINK AND BLUE AISLES

Once parents and caregivers become aware that they should be finding more ways to introduce young girls to STEM content, they often face challenges similar to Eliza's. They may wonder how to choose materials that will engage young girls. Or, they may be wondering if buying pink and purple STEM toys will further perpetuate gender stereotypes. Are there even any truly gender-neutral toys out there?

When walking through the toy section in most department stores, adults are often still confronted with the startling divide between "the pink aisle" and "the blue aisle." Walking through these aisles can feel like stepping into a time machine, warping us into a past era full of masculine and feminine stereotypes we have spent decades trying to eradicate.

In the blue aisle we see sports equipment, action figures, and cars. In the pink aisle we still see baby dolls, dress-up clothes, and toy kitchens. As we saw in chapter 7, there is a long history of marketing gendered toys to children, with STEM toys traditionally being marketed to boys. There has been some shift in this divide recently, with stores like Target announcing that it is creating gender-neutral toy aisles in American stores. Additionally, online retailers and crowdfunding campaign sites like Kickstarter have given birth to a new era of toys that confront typical gender stereotypes.

With so much material to wade through, finding the right STEM tools and products for young girls can be daunting. This chapter will provide you with information about the best types of tools, games, and products currently available that can be used with girls as early as pre-school to practice foundational STEM skills. It will provide you with some examples of specific products, but also arm you with the information needed to select tools to interest young girls regardless of advances in technology or changes to the toy market that happen so rapidly from year to year.

HOW TO CHOOSE STEM TOOLS FOR GIRLS

When choosing STEM tools for girls, it is important to choose tools that engage girls in active problem-solving, hands-on learning, building, and engineering. Remember, it is the *technical* STEM fields, like computer science and engineering, where women are most drastically outnumbered by men. Therefore, remember to choose technologies, digital tools, and applications that teach girls about the human-engineered world beginning in early childhood and continuing through elementary school.

Building kits and materials such as blocks, LEGOs, and DUPLOs are great ways for girls to begin learning about sturdy building and the engineering design process. When considering technologies and apps for young girls, be sure to choose applications that engage girls as *creators* of digital content rather than *consumers* of digital content. Choose tools that prompt girls not to *watch* but to *do*. Instead of just playing a video game about addition, challenge girls to make their own. Programming languages and programmable robotics kits, described in the following sections, are wonderful hands-on ways to introduce girls to technical skills, mathematics, and problem-solving beginning in preschool.

What about color? What about choosing between products marketed to girls versus those marketed to all children or to boys? Forgetting gender stereotypes for just a moment, when it comes to STEM learning, the color or aesthetic design of the tool children are using will not change the concepts they learn. The most important thing is to find out what girls are interested in, and go from there.

In Kelly's case, she was interested in dolls. It made sense for her mom to choose two kits that were relevant to doll play: Emma's Deluxe Bedroom from LEGO Friends, and the Roominate kit. Did that mean Kelly's brother Sam was excluded because the box the parts came in were pink and purple? Absolutely not! He was also interested and was able to join in the fun. Hopefully he even joined in on the doll play once the dollhouse was built. Find out what girls are interested in and build on their interests—regardless of the toy coming from the pink aisle, the blue aisle, or someplace else.

If you are becoming concerned that purchasing only materials featuring pink and purple parts reinforces gender stereotypes, consider integrating these tools with other, more gender-neutral tools. See figure 9.1 for an example of a child's project that uses elements of Roominate materials, LEGOs, and crafts. You can think back to the vignette at the beginning of this chapter when Eliza encourages Kelly to expand on Emma's deluxe bedroom with her other LEGOs and recycled materials found around the house. Encourage boys to play with these pink and purple toys, too! There are also plenty of gender-neutral toys and kits out there. The following sections provide an overview of the many options parents and teachers have to choose from.

PROGRAMMING LANGUAGES

As we saw in part I of this book, computer science–related fields remain heavily masculine. Therefore, engaging girls with programming and computational thinking beginning in early childhood and throughout

Figure 9.1. A child's project that uses elements of the Roominate kit, LEGOs, and more

their academic experience is critical to bridging this gender gap. Be-yond this, it is important for all young children to learn about the technologies that surround them, rather than viewing them as mysterious or working "by magic." From tablets to videogames, smartwatches to traffic lights, coding (a.k.a. computer programming) is all around us.

Many of the human-made objects that children and adults interact with each day run on code. When teaching young children what a program is, adults can explain that a program is a list of instructions that tells a computer, robot, or other technology what to do (see table 9.1 for some key words and child-friendly definitions). That means programs can be used to create video games, websites, animations, and much more!

There are many benefits to introducing computer programming during the early childhood years. For example, programming can foster the

Table 9.1. Young Child–Friendly Technology and Engineering Definitions

Word	Definition	Examples
Program	A list of instructions that tells a robot, computer, or other technology what to do	BEGIN-FORWARD-END is a sample program that tells a KIBO robot to move forward one time
Programming Language	Just like people speak lots of different languages (English, Spanish, French, etc.), different types of technologies speak different languages. A "programming language" is the language that a specific technology understands. Your KIBO robot understands one language (blocks with barcodes) while your Bee-Bot robot understands a different language (arrow keys).	Kids' languages: ScratchJr, Scratch, KIBO blocks Adults' languages: Java, Python, C
Robot	A robot is a special machine that can be programmed to do tasks automatically.	Kids' robots: KIBO, Bee-Bot, Dash, Dot Everyday examples: Roomba
Engineer	A person who designs and builds products, machines, or other objects. They solve problems and make new things that improve our lives.	There are lots of different kinds of engineers! Computer engineers, electrical engineers, aerospace engineers, etc. We can all be engineers (even kids!) when we build models, work on robots, fix and improve things at home, and more.

development of a range of cognitive and social skills. Early studies with the text-based programming language Logo demonstrated that computer programming can help young children with number sense, language skills, and visual memory (Clements, 1999). Computer programming can also help young children practice their developing executive function abilities. Executive functioning consists of mental flexibility, inhibitory control, and working memory (Blair & Diamond, 2008; Shonkoff, Duncan, Fisher, Magnuson, & Raver, 2011). Children as young as 4 years old can learn vital skills of self-expression and cognition through computer programming (Bers, 2018).

Examples of Programming Languages for Young Children

Today, there are a variety of colorful and engaging programming languages designed just for young children. These languages use graphics and symbols (in lieu of text) to teach programming concepts such as sequencing, repeat loops, and conditional statements to young children as early as preschool. For example, the free Daisy the Dinosaur app is designed for young children to practice coding by giving a dinosaur (Daisy) instructions to move and complete simple challenges (figure 9.2). Cargo-Bot is another free app that consists of programming a robot to move crates in order to solve a series of puzzles (figure 9.3).

One of the most popular programming languages for young children is called ScratchJr (figure 9.4). ScratchJr was created through a collaboration between the DevTech Research Group at Tufts University (led by Dr. Marina Umaschi Bers), the Lifelong Kindergarten Group at the MIT Media Lab (led by Dr. Mitchel Resnick), and the Playful Invention Company (led by Paula Bontá and Brian Silverman). It is a free introductory programming language for Chromebooks, iPads, and Android tablets that enables young children (ages five to seven) to create their own interactive stories, collages, and games.

ScratchJr is inspired by Scratch, a free programming environment for older children (ages eight and up) so that developmentally appropriate coding experiences could be available for younger children as well. Using ScratchJr, children snap together graphical blocks to create programs that make characters move, jump, dance, and sing (see figures 9.3 and 9.4). Children can modify the way characters look by using the app's paint editor, or they can draw their own. ScratchJr also provides

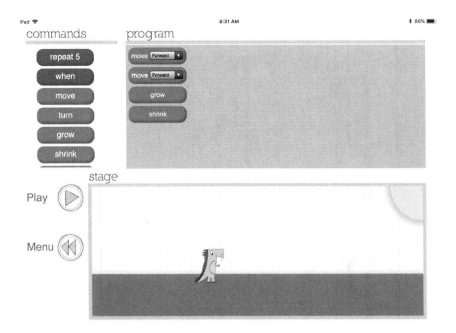

Figure 9.2.   Screenshot of Daisy the Dinosaur

opportunities for children to further personalize their projects by adding in their own voices and sounds, inserting photos of themselves or other objects, drawing their own backgrounds, and more.

ScratchJr is unique among programming apps for young children because it encourages open ended creating, rather than a set series of challenges or levels to complete. Additionally, it was created not only by researchers and technical innovators, but involved collaboration among parents, teachers, and child development specialists. In her book *Coding as a Playground*, Marina Umaschi Bers, one of the cocreators of the ScratchJr app, explains its development:

> We wanted a digital playground to create interactive stories and games using graphical blocks. We wanted to do it right. Therefore, we sought out the best partners available at each stage of development for guidance and valued input, including early childhood educators, parents, principals, and children themselves. (Bers, 2018, p. 117)

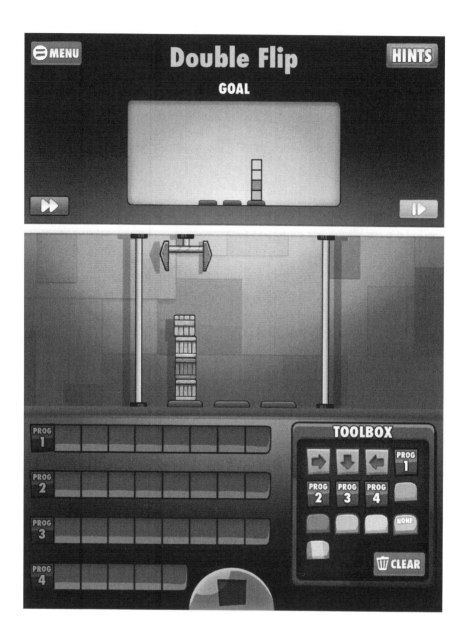

Figure 9.3.   Screenshot of Cargobot

So, what do kids learn with programming languages? Research has shown that children in kindergarten through second grade can success-fully learn foundational programming concepts with ScratchJr (Porte-

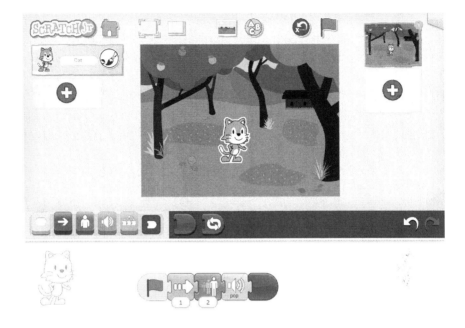

Figure 9.4. Screenshot of ScratchJr

lance & Bers, 2015; Portelance, Strawhacker, & Bers, 2015). Young children are also able to use ScratchJr to create personally meaningful projects and demonstrate computational thinking and problem-solving strategies by using the app (Portelance & Bers, 2015). These problem-solving strategies are useful for young children to learn, even outside a computer programming context.

ROBOTICS KITS

The applications described in the previous section offer a wonderful introduction to coding and problem-solving, but many adults worry (rightfully so) about giving children too much screen time. Programmable robotics kits offer a hands-on introduction to building, engineering, and coding. Hands-on tinkering and building are often missing from the play of young girls. Providing tangible robotics materials can give girls an opportunity to engage in open-ended tinkering and exploring. As an added bonus, many newer robotics kits for young children are programmed with completely screen-free interfaces!

Until recently, educational robotics kits were more often seen in middle and high school environments. Now, educators and researchers know that robotics can offer a range of educational benefits beginning in preschool. Research suggests that children as young as four years old can successfully build and program simple robots while learning a range of engineering concepts in the process (Bers, Ponte, Juelich, Viera, & Schenker, 2002; Cejka, Rogers, & Portsmore, 2006; Kazakoff, Sullivan, & Bers, 2013; Perlman, 1976; Wyeth, 2008). Teaching foundational programming concepts, along with robotics, makes it possible to introduce young children to important ideas that inform the design of many of the everyday objects they interact with (Bers, 2008).

Robotics can also help children develop a stronger understanding of mathematical concepts such as number, size, and shape in much the same way that traditional materials like pattern blocks, beads, and balls do (Brosterman, 1997; Resnick et al., 1998). Unlike many other types of educational technologies, robotics activities do not involve sitting alone in front of a screen. Instead, robotic manipulatives allow children to socialize and collaborate while developing fine motor skills and hand-eye coordination.

Examples of Early Childhood Robotics Kits

There are several robotics kits now on the commercial market specifically designed for young learners. One popular robot for young children, called Bee-Bot (figure 9.5), is designed to look like a colorful bee. It is easily programmed with directional keys on the Bee-Bot's back, and children can enter up to 40 commands. The commands direct Bee-Bot forward, backward, left, and right. After selecting the commands, pressing the green GO button starts Bee-Bot on its way. Bee-Bot blinks and beeps at the conclusion of each command to allow children to follow Bee-Bot through the program they have entered, and then confirms its completion with lights and sound.

Robots like Bee-Bot offer a wonderful hands-on alternative to the screen-based programming languages described in the previous section. Children can talk and collaborate while programming Bee-Bot to navigate around the room, around obstacles, or along one of the many floor

Figure 9.5.   Bee-Bot robot programmed with directional keys on its back

maps that are sold to accompany the robot. However, Bee-Bot is a
robot that is already built and constructed. It does not engage children
in building or engineering the same way that robotics kits for older
children do.

When looking for a robotics kit that will engage young girls in both
building and programming, kits like the KIBO Robotics Kit (available
for purchase at www.kinderlabrobotics.com) offer the best of both
worlds. KIBO is a robotics kit designed to playfully introduce young
children (ages four to seven) to foundational engineering and programming concepts through tangible screen-free activities. KIBO was created based on research by Marina Umaschi Bers and the Developmental
Technologies Research Group at Tufts University, and made commercially available by KinderLab Robotics through funding from the National Science Foundation (NSF) and a successful Kickstarter campaign.

Unlike its counterparts on the commercial market, KIBO engages
children in both building with robotic parts (KIBO's hardware) and

programming KIBO to move with tangible programming blocks (KIBO's software). KIBO is designed based on years of child development research at Tufts University, and is explicitly intended to meet the developmental needs of young children (e.g., Kazakoff & Bers, 2014; Sullivan & Bers, 2016; Sullivan, Elkin, & Bers, 2015). The kit contains easy-to-connect construction materials including wheels, motors, light output, a variety of sensors, and wooden art platforms (figure 9.6).

KIBO is programmed to move using a tangible programming language that consists of interlocking wooden programming blocks (figure 9.7). KIBO's core language consists of 18 blocks and 12 parameters.

Figure 9.6.   The KIBO robot and sample block program

With just 18 blocks, children are able to master increasingly complex programming concepts such as repeat loops, conditional statements, and nesting statements. The wooden blocks resemble familiar early childhood manipulatives such as alphabet blocks, and contain no embedded electronics or digital components. KIBO's body has an embedded scanner that scans the barcodes on the programming blocks one at a time. Once the program has been scanned, it is instantly saved on the robot, and KIBO will perform the program with the press of a button. Like Bee-Bot, no interaction with a computer, tablet, or other screen-based software is required to learn programming with KIBO. Beyond the core 18 blocks, KinderLab Robotics continues to offer new programming blocks that expand on KIBO's capabilities each year.

Kits like KIBO are perfect for young girls for a few key reasons. First, KIBO is designed for open-ended play that allows girls to make almost anything they want based on their own personal interests. KIBO can be used to act out a scene from a story or movie; it can be decorated

Figure 9.7. KIBO's block programming language

to look like an animal; it can become a carousel or a fire truck. There-fore, KIBO can be used to help a young girl explore almost any interest.

Second, KIBO has a neutral aesthetic, making it equally appealing to children of any gender. With so few truly gender-neutral toys out there, this is a plus for parents and educators who want a tool that will appeal to many children. Finally, KIBO engages girls in hands-on building and tinkering as well as programming. Opportunities to tinker and engineer is a critical piece of engaging girls with STEM in early childhood and setting them up for success down the line.

BOARD GAMES, BUILDING KITS, AND MORE

One downside of robotics kits is that the good ones tend to be more expensive than other toys and games for young children. However, there are many other types of kits and games that adults can look for to engage young girls with STEM. For example, providing girls with gen-eral building manipulatives such as LEGOs, DUPLOs, blocks, and re-cycled materials can be a wonderful way to have girls tinker, problem-solve, build, and create. You probably already have many of these mate-rials lying around your classroom or playroom. Chapter 10 will give examples of the types of curricular activities that adults can implement at home and at school to use these everyday materials to kick-start a girl's mathematical and engineering mindset.

For those hoping to teach coding without the use of screen-based apps or expensive robots, adding a coding-themed board game into choice time at school or a family game night at home can be a fun and collaborative way to engage girls with computer science principles. For example, Robot Turtles is a board game for children ages four and up to practice programming skills (figure 9.8). In this game, children use programming instruction cards to navigate their turtle around obstacles in order to reach their jewel. The board can be set up differently each time the game is played, allowing players to customize how challenging the game is and also adding many opportunities to play again and again without it feeling repetitive. Board games like Robot Turtles are a great choice because these are social, allowing multiple children to play to-gether and/or children to play along with an adult.

STEM PRODUCTS DESIGNED FOR GIRLS

So far this chapter has provided examples of STEM products that are designed and marketed in a gender-neutral fashion. With the gender disparity in STEM fields reaching the national spotlight, there has been a push to design STEM toys specifically marketed to young girls. For example, the company GoldieBlox, which first emerged in 2012, creates toys, books, apps, videos, animations, and other merchandise that foster engineering, spatial reasoning, and problem-solving, centered on female characters to engage girls.

The founder and CEO of GoldieBlox, Stanford-educated engineer Debbie Sterling, launched the company with the goal of disrupting the pink aisle. But beyond pink and purple packaging, GoldieBlox aims to appeal to girls through incorporating a story narrative component. Debbie Sterling explained this goal in a 2016 interview with *Business Insider*, saying "girls really love stories and narratives . . . it became really obvious to me that the way to get girls engaged in engineering and

Figure 9.8.   The Robot Turtles board game

building was to incorporate a narrative" (Loudenback, 2016). The company's first product, for girls ages four and up, introduced the character of Goldie through a storybook and construction set while engaging girls with building a belt drive.

Similarly, Roominate offers a line of STEM-focused building toys specifically marketed to girls by playing on the idea of dollhouses. Roominate kits offer girls circuits, motors, and modular building pieces to build and create interactive rooms, dollhouses, vehicles, or their own unique structures that can be joined together or taken apart.

The LEGO Friends line, launched in 2012, also offers a series of building kits marketed to girls that can be used to practice building, engineering, and tinkering. LEGO Friends kits include mini doll figures and LEGO pieces in pink-and-purple color schemes that depict scenes from suburban life set in the fictional town of Heartlake City.

While these kits can be used with children of any gender, they are skillfully marketed to girls with traditionally "feminine" color schemes and aesthetics. Girls are featured in the ads for these products, and often on the boxes themselves. These kits also appeal to girls by featuring female characters and role models and capitalizing on girls' interest in storytelling and doll play.

It is important to reach girls with STEM tools that appeal to their interests and hobbies. This growing crop of girl-powered STEM kits offer new ways to reach girls (or any children) who may not have been interested in traditional STEM toys such as robots and planes. For example, the newest company to join this crew of girl-powered STEM products is Joulez. Joulez is targeted to elementary children ages eight through twelve, and aims to create fashionable gadgets and technologies that fuse together fashion, crafts, and electronic kits (see www. joulez.co).

In an interview for this book with Stephanie Rowe, the CEO of Joulez, Rowe discusses why it is important to design and create products that will specifically engage girls, rather than taking a more gender-neutral approach. "I don't see this as designing products *just* for girls," Rowe says. "I see this as designing beyond the default." Rowe describes the "default" STEM products as helicopters, robots, and drones. These products only reach a specific type of child. In order to reach a more diverse range of children—girls or children of any gender that simply don't enjoy the default STEM products out there—Rowe creates STEM products that involve fashion, arts, decorating, and more.

RECOMMENDATIONS FOR ADULTS

We've seen that there are a wide variety of toys, robots, games, apps, and building kits that are available to begin incorporating STEM skills into girls' everyday play. Seeing all the choices may be even more overwhelming for adults who aren't sure where to begin. Here are a few tips to guide you as you take a stroll through the toy aisle:

- Provide girls with tools that allow them to tinker, build, practice spatial reasoning, and engineer (examples: blocks, LEGOs, DUPLOs, recycled materials).
- Provide girls with tools that engage them in computer science–related play (examples: programming apps and programmable robotics kits).
- Provide girls with tools that allow them to work or play with other children (examples: STEM board games and tangible building and robotics kits).
- Provide girls with tools and toys that work with their hobbies and interests, whether they come from the pink aisle, blue aisle, or any other aisle! If you are worried that the packaging/marketing of a toy will make girls shy away, then toss the box before you offer them the toy.

Picking out STEM tools is only one part of the challenge adults face. Girls must also *use* these tools (more than once!) for them to make an impact. That means adults must find ways to engage girls with these tools in ways that playfully foster STEM learning. The next chapter will discuss how to create hands-on activities and curricula that engage young girls using tools such as the ones mentioned in this chapter.

REFERENCES

Bers, M. U. (2008). *Blocks, robots and computers: Learning about technology in early childhood.* New York: Teacher's College Press.

Bers, M. U. (2018). *Coding as a Playground: Programming and Computational Thinking in the Early Childhood Classroom.* New York, NY: Routledge.

Bers, M. U., Ponte, I., Juelich, C., Viera, A., & Schenker, J. (2002). Teachers as designers: Integrating robotics in early childhood education. *Information Technology in Childhood Education Annual, 2002*(1), 123–145.

Blair, C., & Diamond, A. (2008). Biological processes in prevention and intervention: The promotion of self-regulation as a means of preventing school failure. *Development and psychopathology, 20*(3), 899–911.

Brosterman, N. (1997). *Inventing kindergarten.* New York: H. N. Abrams.

Cejka, E., Rogers, C., & Portsmore, M. (2006). Kindergarten robotics: Using robotics to motivate math, science, and engineering literacy in elementary school. *International Journal of Engineering Education, 22*(4), 711.

Clements, D. (1999). The future of educational computing research: the case of computer programming. *Information Technology in Childhood Education Annual,* 147–179.

Kazakoff, E. R., & Bers, M. U. (2014). Put your robot in, put your robot out: Sequencing through programming robots in early childhood. *Journal of Educational Computing Research, 50*(4). Retrieved from https://sites.tufts.edu/devtech/files/2018/02/Kazakoff-Put-Your-Robot-In.pdf

Kazakoff, E., Sullivan, A., & Bers, M. U. (2013). The effect of a classroom-based intensive robotics and programming workshop on sequencing ability in early childhood. *Early Childhood Education Journal, 41*(4), 245–255. DOI=10.1007/s10643-012-0554-5.

Loudenback, T. (2016, June 15). This company's toys are helping mold in a new generation of engineers. *Business Insider.* Retrieved from www.businessinsider.com/goldieblox-ceo-debbie-sterling-2016-5

Portelance, D. J., & Bers, M. U. (2015, June). Code and tell: Assessing young children's learning of computational thinking using peer video interviews with ScratchJr. In *Proceedings of the 14th International Conference on Interaction Design and Children (IDC '15),* 271–274. Boston, MA: Association for Computing Machinery.

Portelance, D. J., Strawhacker, A., & Bers, M. U. (2015). Constructing the ScratchJr programming language in the early childhood classroom. *International Journal of Technology and Design Education,* 1–16.

Resnick, M., Martin, F., Berg, R., Borovoy, R., Colella, V., Kramer, K., & Silverman, B. (1998, April). Digital manipulatives. In *Proceedings of the CHI '98 conference,* 281–287. Los Angeles, CA: ACM Press.

Perlman, R. (1976). *Using computer technology to provide a creative learning environment for preschool children* [Logo memo no. 24]. Cambridge, MA: MIT Artificial Intelligence Laboratory Publications 260.

Shonkoff, J. P., Duncan, G. J., Fisher, P. A., Magnuson, K., & Raver, C. (2011). Building the brain's "air traffic control" system: How early experiences shape the development of executive function. *Contract, 11.*

Sullivan, A., & Bers, M. U. (2016). Robotics in the early childhood classroom: Learning outcomes from an 8-week robotics curriculum in pre-kindergarten through second grade. *International Journal of Technology and Design Education, 26*(1), 3–20.

Sullivan, A., Elkin, M., & Bers, M. U. (2015). KIBO robot demo: Engaging young children in programming and engineering. In *Proceedings of the 14th International Conference on Interaction Design and Children (IDC '15),* 418–421. Boston, MA: ACM Press.

Wyeth, P. (2008). How young children learn to program with sensor, action, and logic blocks. *International Journal of the Learning Sciences, 17*(4), 517–550.

10

CREATE ENGAGING STEM ACTIVITIES FOR YOUNG GIRLS

DESIGNING EARLY CHILDHOOD STEM CURRICULA

This chapter will provide guidance on creating engaging STEM curricula and activities for young children that can be used with girls in schools, homes, camps, and extracurricular settings. It will provide specific curricular suggestions for appealing to the interests of girls, but all of the topics and approaches presented are also beneficial when used with all children. Of course, educators will need to follow their own state curricular frameworks and school-specific policies when it comes to exact math, science, and engineering content knowledge that must be taught at each grade level. Thinking beyond these specific requirements, early childhood is a time to help frame children's interests, mindsets, and approaches. This chapter focuses on strategies for designing curricula that does the following for young girls:

- Fosters interest in STEM areas
- Encourages scientific inquiry
- Provides time for tinkering and building
- Provides time for meaningful explorations
- Showcases diverse STEM role models
- Provides chances for safe risk-taking and making mistakes

The goal of quality STEM curricula in early childhood education should not be simply drilling content knowledge or facts. It should be nurturing children's interests and curiosity about the way the world works. It should focus on instilling confidence and positive attitudes toward STEM subjects. This is true for all children, but especially for girls and other students who are underrepresented in STEM fields.

ACTIVITIES AND LESSONS THAT APPEAL TO GIRLS

In order to instill confidence and positive attitudes towards STEM in young girls, educators must first create activities in which girls will enjoy participating. Where does this leave boys or children who identify as other genders? Well, the same strategies that research has shown to be appealing to girls can benefit all children, regardless of gender. For example, while many extracurricular STEM clubs and programs focus on competition, which is typically conceptualized as masculine (such as popular robotics competitions and leagues), research has shown that girls may excel more in collaborative environments as compared to competitive ones (Gneezy & Rustichini, 2004). Women and girls tend to avoid competitive work environments, and tend to perform worse than men when placed in those environments (Gneezy, Niederle, & Rustichini, 2003; Gneezy & Rustichini, 2004; Niederle & Vesterlund, 2007).

While there is some evidence that competition may improve boys' performance on certain tasks, there are many benefits to collaborative learning for any individual. For example, collaborative learning projects allow opportunities for peers to identify and fill gaps in one another's knowledge, and stimulate deeper individual knowledge (Van Boxtel, Van der Linden, & Kanselaar, 2000).

In order to properly support girls' exploration of STEM, educators and parents should consider the following five guidelines when designing STEM activities:

1. *Collaboration:* Girls typically benefit from collaboration and a chance to work together or discuss ideas. Choose collaborative STEM projects over competitive ones whenever possible. Examples of collaborative STEM projects include things like working

in pairs to design and program a robot that dances the hokey-pokey, cultivating a kindergarten class garden, or getting the whole family together to build a LEGO bridge and test its strength. Or, present collaborative projects as another option in addition to competitive, league-based STEM activities.

2. *Personally meaningful projects:* Girls will learn STEM material best when they are completing projects that feel relevant to them and are personally meaningful. Try to allow girls an opportunity to create projects to that are important to them, rather than exploring an abstract concept or theme. For example, instead of having an entire class create animated collages about the same book, have children choose their favorite book and make a digital project about it.

3. *Hands-on exploration:* Girls need exposure to activities that allow them to tinker, build, and explore through hands-on and open-ended projects and playtime. Research has shown that building and tinkering during one's childhood is beneficial in an engineering career later in life, and that women often have less experience with childhood tinkering than men. STEM curricula for girls should attempt to address this gap by providing materials and activities that encourage tinkering.

4. *Female role models:* Projects should allow girls to be exposed to successful females in STEM areas. They should be able to learn from female mentors and imagine themselves in their shoes. If you are a female educator, remember that *you* are a powerful STEM role model, regardless of your career. The way you model scientific curiosity, a joy for engineering and building, and confidence in these areas are powerful for young girls to see.

5. *Projects that instill confidence:* Activities should give girls chances to gain confidence in their STEM skills and abilities. Be sure to celebrate milestones (big and small) throughout the entire process of any STEM project you explore. Remember, the final product is not the only milestone to celebrate! Parents and teachers should remember to provide positive feedback on things girls can control, such as their effort, their problem-solving strategies, or their behavior and attitude throughout the project.

FROM STEM TO STEAM

Thus far in this book, we have been focusing on the acronym "STEM." Over the past few years, there has been growing enthusiasm from educators and researchers for a newer acronym, "STEAM," which involves integrating the *arts* ("A") with STEM in educational settings. This trend has been emerging in school curricula, new educational initiatives, and even in popular children's media such as *Sesame Street.* In the 43rd season of *Sesame Street,* the television show continued its STEM education with the addition of arts, introducing young children to the acronym STEAM for the first time (Maeda, 2012).

Infusing the "A" of arts in STEAM means integrating the visual arts, culture, music, social studies, and more within STEM projects and classes. There are many benefits to the STEAM approach. For example, adding the arts to STEM-based subjects, such as computer programming and engineering, may enhance student learning by infusing opportunities for creativity and innovation (Robelen, 2011). You may be surprised to learn that many modern innovations that we rely on each day have resulted from the integration of the arts with STEM. For example, the computer chips that run almost all of our digital devices are made using a combination of three classic artistic inventions: etching, silkscreen printing, and photolithography (Root-Bernstein, 2011).

From Leonardo Da Vinci to Frank Lloyd Wright, many of our most beloved STEM heroes were often artists as well. It is estimated that Nobel laureates in the sciences are 17 times likelier than the average scientist to be a painter, 12 times as likely to be a poet, and 4 times as likely to be a musician (Pomeroy, 2012). This is likely because the arts, like science, technology, engineering, and mathematics, are rooted in a similar mindset of curiosity, innovation, and creativity.

Beyond the benefits already stated, the STEAM approach offers a new way to attract the interest of students who are not traditionally drawn to math, science, and engineering. Many girls are interested in liberal arts fields like art, dance, music, and drama. Therefore, STEAM projects offer a new avenue for these girls to get involved with technical projects that may not interest them otherwise. By integrating the arts with technical and scientific fields starting in early childhood, young children grow up with the abilities they need to be well-rounded thinkers in any domain they pursue. The following section will provide examples of STEAM curricula to engage girls in scientific and technical play and exploration.

STEAM CURRICULUM: WHAT DOES IT LOOK LIKE?

What exactly does STEAM curriculum look like in practice? Table 10.1 provides examples of tried and true STEAM curriculum units that are perfect for engaging young girls in science, math, and engineering through a liberal arts lens.

The curriculum ideas presented in table 10.1 can be implemented slowly over the course of many months or more quickly based on the students' prior experience and readiness. Each curriculum idea could be presented as a one-time STEM activity, as a deep-dive final project, or as an incremental curriculum that builds on concepts one at a time in 45-minute to one-hour sessions once a week. Pacing and progression will depend on children's developmental readiness as well as logistics including materials available, amount of time available, number of children, and number of adults available to help facilitate the activity. When planning the logistics of your curriculum, go through the following steps (see appendix C for a curriculum planning sheet based on these steps):

1. *Topic:* Choose a STEAM topic to explore. Consider the learning goals for exploring this topic. What learning domains or content areas does it cover? Does it align with any frameworks or standards?
2. *Time:* How much time will you have to devote to exploring this topic? Will you have this time all at once or in small increments? What can reasonably be covered given your time constraints? Answering this question will help you decide how to explore the topic you've chosen.
3. *Preparation:* What will you need to prepare to teach this? Will you need extra training yourself? Give yourself a suitable amount of time to play with any new materials and gain confidence in your own STEAM skills before leading an activity.
4. *Audience:* Who will be completing this curriculum? Take time to consider their age, interests, and developmental needs. Will this

Table 10.1. STEAM Curriculum Examples

Curriculum	Content Areas	Description
Dances from Around the World	Robotics, Engineering, Music, Dance, Culture	This curriculum unit (originally designed by the DevTech Research Group and adapted by many schools and teachers) involves the integration of music and culture with engineering and robotics. It culminates with students programming their KIBO robot to perform a dance they have learned about (hula, samba, the lion dance, and more!). Robots are decorated in the theme of the chosen dance, and students learn to dance along with their robots in a final recital.
Fairy Tale STEM	Engineering, Storytelling, Literacy, Math	Fairy tale STEM activities are a popular way to combine literature and storytelling with STEM. Revisit classic tales such as *The Three Little Pigs* and have students build their own houses out of wooden popsicle sticks, plastic straws, or LEGO bricks. Test these houses out against the "Big Bad Wolf" (i.e., a powerful fan with multiple settings). Or, explore fairy tales like *Cinderella* and *Rapunzel* and build creations to help the characters create their own happy endings. For example, what if Rapunzel built a ladder? How long would it need to be? And how could we make it sturdy enough?
My Family Digital Collage	Technology, Engineering, Art, Identity	Using a programming language like ScratchJr, students can combine art, programming, and an exploration of family and identity by programming an interactive collage! The digital collage should include images and animations that represent the student's family, culture, and background.
Class Garden	Science, Math, Technology, Art, Writing	Growing a class garden is hands-on way for young children to learn about how plants grow while practicing observation skills, measurement, and more. There are lots of different types of DIY seed starter pots you can explore: eggshells, K-cups, and more! Turn the garden into a full-fledged science experiment by trying out different types of pots and seeing which are most effective at growing your seeds. Involve measurement to keep track of how the plants grow. Use technology to record and document pictures and videos and to animate plant life cycles. Integrate the visual arts by decorating the pots and the class garden area. This project can even integrate writing as kids journal about their plants' growth.

curriculum be completed by just girls? Or will it be used with children of all genders?

5. *Activities:* Now that you have outlined your learnings goals and have spent time thinking about your audience, it is time to think about what exactly you will be doing to address these learning

goals. What activities will you complete? Refer back to step 2 to make sure you have enough time to complete the activities you are designing.

6. *Materials and logistics:* Once you've outlined your activities, take a moment to plan for any final logistics or special arrangements. Think about all the materials you will need and how you will disperse them (e.g., Will students work in pairs and share materials? Will there be enough materials for everyone to work independently?).

HOW (AND WHERE) TO MAKE IT HAPPEN

Now that you have seen examples of STEAM curriculum projects and know the steps to creating your own, you may be wondering about the logistics of making these projects happen in your home, school, museum, or other early childhood setting. There are many ways to get started! Here are a few suggestions:

- *Take a field trip.* If you are not quite ready to begin teaching your own full-fledged STEAM curriculum unit, consider visiting a space in the community to immerse your young child/children in science and engineering. Science museums and makerspaces are great places to start. Many local universities have makerspaces or tech labs, and are happy to host a field trip or tour. Use the field trip to come up with ideas to explore further at home or at school.

- *Get outside.* Exploring parks, trails, forests, ponds, wildlife refuges, and other outdoor spaces are also a great way to start scientific exploration with young children. Even your backyard or school field will do! Getting kids out into nature prompts them to immediately explore their surroundings and fosters their sense of exploration and curiosity. While outside, ask questions, encourage exploration (e.g., safely taking a close look at plants, leaves, animals), and provide opportunities for documentation to return to later (e.g., pictures, notes, drawings). If you don't have access to these types of natural areas, consider planting a small garden or even simply growing seeds in cups!

- *Involve parents and family members.* STEAM projects that involve technologies like robotics or other electronics can be a lot for a teacher or parent to implement on their own, at least at first. Kids can sometimes have a lot of questions and demand the adult's attention all at once. This can be overwhelming for one person to manage alone, especially if embarking on this for the first time. It can be helpful for teachers to ask for parent or family volunteers to come and help facilitate your lesson or project. Even if they are not subject matter experts, they can help manage kids' frustrations and resolve interpersonal conflicts. Or, you may discover that within your parent network, there are many scientists and engineers you didn't even know about! They may jump at the chance to lead a lesson for you.
- *Collaborate across disciplines.* STEAM work is about collaboration and innovation across disciplines. STEAM projects are a great way to involve the expertise of art teachers, science teachers, and math teachers. Draw on the experience and expertise of your colleagues to make your STEAM project a reality.

When it comes to *where* this STEAM learning should happen, you have many options. Beyond exploring outside, your own home or classroom is probably a perfect place to start. By adding in simple supplies such as blocks and building materials, you could easily create a STEAM learning corner in your classroom, playroom, or living room. Schools that have libraries, computer labs, or makerspaces for older children may also benefit from having an early childhood section or wing added on.

THINK BEYOND THE SCHOOL DAY

It is important to think about providing girls with STEAM curricular activities beyond the confines of the school day. School days are jam-packed with requirements and standard curricular goals that must be met. While STEAM tools and activities can be a nice means to cover a great deal of required curricular content, sometimes it is just not feasible for teachers to implement all of the wonderful and engaging STEAM projects that we know would benefit girls.

Additionally, since most school environments are coeducational, it can be difficult to implement any initiatives directly targeted to girls. Luckily, there are many extracurricular programs that parents and educators can encourage girls to join, beginning in early elementary school. For example, LEGO robotics leagues such as FIRST LEGO League Jr. (grades K–4) and FIRST LEGO League (grades 4–8) offer a way to get involved with engineering and robotics beginning in elementary school. Even traditional extracurricular programs for girls, such as the Girl Scouts, are now offering ways for girls to engage with STEM. Through partnerships and sponsorships, the Girl Scouts now offer several badges that focus on building STEM skills, including: Naturalist, Digital Art, Science & Technology, and Innovation badges.

Parents, librarians, and educators can come up with their own extracurricular clubs, activities, and programs to playfully introduce young girls to STEAM content. Consider the following ideas to get started:

- *Girls coding club:* If you are looking to reach girls, sometimes the best approach is to create a girls-only environment. Starting a coding club at your school, community center, or library is a great way to create a safe place for girls to explore coding beginning in early elementary school! Many coding applications are free (ScratchJr is a great place to start) and have free online educational resources and curricular ideas as well. Allow girls to work together to create projects that they are interested in, and provide frequent opportunities to showcase their work and build their confidence. If funding is available, consider exploring coding with apps, robots, board games, and more (refer to the previous chapter for more ideas).

- *Mommy & Me STEAM:* For moms who are looking to engage their kids with STEAM content, consider creating a Mommy & Me STEAM group. It will be good for both young girls *and* young boys to see their mothers (i.e., their ultimate female role model!) displaying interest and confidence while learning and exploring engineering and science topics with their children. Moms can take turns leading a project each month.

- *STEAM Saturdays:* Exploring science, math, and technology can sometimes be more playful and fun outside the confines of the school day. Consider starting a STEAM Saturday series and explore a different topic or tool each weekend. You won't need to worry as much about timing or assessments as you would during a normal school day. Saturday sessions can also be longer than the typical amount of time you have to devote to one subject during the school day. This allows plenty of time for tinkering and free play along with guided projects or challenges.

- *STEM Girl Buddies:* Girls need to see female role models succeeding in STEM. But these role models don't need to be professional scientists or engineers; they can be girls just a few grades above them in school! Consider a mentorship program in which girls in older grades come to teach girls in younger grades about a particular science, engineering, or coding topic. It will be powerful for young girls to learn from older female peers.

DESIGNING GENDER-INCLUSIVE CURRICULA

You are now armed with the knowledge you need to create fun and engaging STEM and STEAM curricula and extracurricular programs for young girls. Remember that regardless of what you teach or how you are teaching it, it is important to design gender-inclusive curricula and use-inclusive teaching practices. Once you have designed your curriculum or lesson plan, use table 10.2 to take a quick check on how inclusive your plans are. If you said "yes" to most of the statements in the table, you are on the right track to engage children of all genders with the STEM topics you are exploring. If you answered "no" or "maybe," then consider investing some time in checking through your curriculum and lesson plans, and making the necessary changes before trying it out with kids.

Table 10.2.   Gender-Inclusive STEM Teaching Checklist

Teacher Statements	Yes	No	Maybe
I have taken a close look at my curriculum materials to identify and remove any possible gender stereotyping.	☐	☐	☐
The topics and examples I have chosen will equally appeal to all my students, regardless of gender.	☐	☐	☐
My teaching plan will promote equal opportunities for all my students, regardless of gender.	☐	☐	☐

Women and men are explicitly presented as being equally capable and successful in STEM-related fields.	☐	☐	☐
Female and male role models are provided when teaching about STEM-related professions.	☐	☐	☐

REFERENCES

Gneezy, U., Niederle, M., & Rustichini, A. (2003). Performance in competitive environments: Gender differences. *Quarterly Journal of Economics, 118*(3), 1049–1074.

Gneezy, U., & Rustichini, A. (2004). Gender and competition at a young age. *American Economic Review, 94*(2), 377–381.

Maeda, J. (2012, October 2). STEM to STEAM: Art in K–12 is key to building a strong economy. *Edutopia: What works in education.* Retrieved from https://www.edutopia.org/blog/stem-to-steam-strengthens-economy-john-maeda

Niederle, M., & Vesterlund, L. (2007). Do women shy away from competition? Do men compete too much? *Quarterly Journal of Economics, 122*(3), 1067–1101.

Pomeroy, S. R. (2012, August 22). From STEM to STEAM: Science and art go hand in hand. *Scientific American Guest Blog.* Retrieved from https://blogs.scientificamerican.com/guest-blog/from-stem-to-steam-science-and-the-arts-go-hand-in-hand/

Robelen, E. W. (2011). STEAM: Experts make case for adding arts to STEM. *Education Week, 31*(13), 8.

Root-Bernstein, R. (2011, April). The art of scientific and technological innovations. *Science-Blogs.* Retrieved from https://scienceblogs.com/art_of_science_learning/2011/04/11/the-art-of-scientific-and-tech-1

Van Boxtel, C., Van der Linden, J., & Kanselaar, G. (2000). Collaborative learning tasks and the elaboration of conceptual knowledge. *Learning and Instruction, 10*(4), 311–330.

11

SIMPLE THINGS ADULTS CAN DO

Over the course of this book, we have explored some serious and, often, disheartening topics. We have examined the perpetuation of gender stereotypes in our culture and their influence on our children. We have also seen startling statistics about the persistent gender disparity between men and women in STEM career fields, particularly technology and engineering fields. At this point, you might be asking yourselves: what is there to be done?

The good news is there are many things that can be done! In fact, simply by investing your time in exploring this topic you have taken the first step: educating yourself about the impact of stereotypes. In addition to arming yourself with knowledge, this chapter provides several practical steps that parents, teachers, and other caregivers can take in order to break STEM stereotypes and set up girls for success.

START YOUNG AND CONTINUE STRONG

The previous chapters have outlined the many reasons why early experiences are important. Exposure to biased media and experiences with gender stereotypes that happen during early childhood can have a lasting impact on girls' interests, hobbies, and identity development as they grow up. It is important not to wait until girls are choosing high school courses or thinking about college majors to engage them with STEM content.

We are lucky to live in a time when there are amazing toys, technologies, and resources to teach STEM, beginning in preschool (refer back to chapter 9 for ideas). Educators and caregivers should take advantage of these tools and make playful exploration of STEM content a part of every young girl's early childhood upbringing. Providing an early foundation of STEM knowledge will arm girls with the skills to pursue these subjects throughout elementary school, middle school, and beyond.

In addition to starting young with teaching STEM concepts and skills, educators and caregivers must be aware of the role models and media messages that girls receive beginning in early childhood. We must consider improving girls' self-confidence and interest in STEM, not just their competence. We must be aware of stereotypes we are perpetuating around young children, before we even think these children are old enough to pick up on what we are saying. Therefore, for each of the following tips and suggestions presented in this chapter, remember: *start young!*

This is not to say that we can forget about interventions that take place in middle school, high school, college, and the professional arena. The gender disparity in STEM is a big and complex problem. It cannot be fixed by placing a band-aid or patch weld on any one place in the STEM pipeline, and early childhood interventions are certainly not meant to be a "cure all" solution. Interventions should support girls and women at *all* stages in their journey along the STEM pipeline. We must start young and continue strong until we see a real shift in these male-dominated fields.

INFORM OTHERS ABOUT STEREOTYPES AND STEREOTYPE THREAT

By reading this book, you have taken a critical first step in addressing a big piece of the problem: you have armed yourself with knowledge and awareness of gender stereotypes and stereotype threat. Without knowledge of this problem, there is no way to enact change. Therefore, it is critical that parents, teachers, and caregivers are informed about the gender divide in STEM fields and the role of stereotypes so that they can work together to tackle this problem at home, at school, and in extracurricular settings.

So how do you get the word out? Consider circulating a factsheet about the gender divide in STEM and the impact of stereotypes (see appendix A for a sample factsheet) with your fellow parents, teachers, or colleagues. Make this issue an important one that is brought up at teacher meetings, PTA meetings, curriculum planning sessions, and parent meetups. Provide your peers and colleagues with the suggestions from this chapter so that they can begin to make changes in their practice with young children.

In addition to informing other adults, it is also helpful to teach children about the impact of stereotypes. Research shows that teaching about stereotype threat may be one way to reduce its influence on stigmatized groups (Johns, Schmader, & Martens, 2005). This can be done in different ways depending on the age of the children with whom you are working.

When working with very young children, parents or teachers can foster a discussion around stereotypes as they emerge. For example, if a teacher hears someone say that "the LEGOs are for the boys," this might be discussed later during circle time by saying, "Does anyone else believe that certain toys in the classroom are just for the boys or just for the girls? What makes you think that?" Be sure to reinforce that all the toys and tools in the classroom or playroom (including trucks, dolls, LEGOs, and robots) are there for *all* children to play with, regardless of gender.

If you encounter a gender stereotype while reading a picture book, be sure you address it with children rather than gloss over it. For example, if you encounter a story where all the engineers are boys, be sure to prompt kids with questions like, "Do you think this means there are no girl engineers? Tomorrow, should we read a book with female engineers to remind us that isn't true?"

When working with older children, beginning in elementary school and throughout middle school, it may be appropriate to more explicitly teach about the impact of stereotypes. You may wish to define the word "stereotypes" for students and have them discuss stereotypes they have (or are aware of from the media or elsewhere) about boys and girls. A simple definition of stereotypes you can share would be "something that we believe to be true about a particular group of people, that is often untrue." When discussing stereotypes with kids, ask prompting questions such as:

- Where do you think these stereotypes come from?
- What are your personal experiences with stereotypes?
- Where do we see these stereotypes in books, on TV, or in advertising?
- How might these stereotypes be limiting?
- How can we make positive changes in order to break these stereotypes?

By providing opportunities to discuss and address stereotypes, students will be less likely to act on them in the future.

FOSTER A GROWTH MINDSET

Personal views about intelligence and failure may also impact girls' achievement and long-term persistence in rigorous STEM fields. Psychologist Carol Dweck spent decades researching achievement and success and developed the concept of the "growth mindset" (Dweck, 2002; 2008). The "growth mindset" is the belief that intelligence is not fixed, but instead can change and grow incrementally through practice.

Dweck demonstrated that students who see intelligence as fixed (a "fixed mindset") are less likely to show persistence in subjects or fields in which they do not think they have the intelligence necessary to succeed. In contrast, students with a growth mindset (who see intelligence as malleable) are more likely to persist and strive to achieve their goals in fields in which they may not already see themselves as highly competent. Prior work has also found that women were more likely to label lack of ability (rather than lack of motivation) as the cause of their failures (Dweck, Goetz, & Strauss, 1980). If girls and women think about intelligence with a growth mindset, they may be less likely to be discouraged or dissuaded from continuing to pursue challenging STEM-focused degrees and careers.

One of the biggest actions that parents and educators can take to foster a growth mindset in young children is learning to praise the right way. Instead of simply telling kids they are smart or gifted, which implies they were born this way and does not encourage growth, praise their effort. Praise the time and hard work children put into their project or in mastering a new skill, rather than just the outcome.

While offering praise like "you are so smart!" may offer a self-esteem boost in the short term, over the long term it makes children lose confidence when tasks become hard. Consider nuanced praise, such as "I am so impressed that you spent so many hours working hard on this robot and even continued working hard when you had trouble figuring out how to attach those motors!" Not only does this type of praise help to foster the growth mindset, but it also shows you are paying close attention to their work, rather than offering cookie-cutter compliments.

In addition to changing the way educators and caregivers praise children, there are other simple actions that can help foster a growth mindset. Try to convey the following:

- *The brain works like a muscle.* Remind children that the brain can only grow through hard work and lots of practice. Tell them, "You have to train your brain!"
- *Embrace mistakes and failures along the way.* Mistakes are opportunities to grow and are a big part of the learning process—especially in STEM!
- *Embrace the power of "yet."* If kids express they can't do something or they aren't good at something, reframe this with the word "yet." Remind them to say, "I can't do this *yet*" or "I haven't figured out this math problem *yet*" rather than giving up. This encourages perseverance amidst challenging tasks.

PLAY THE RIGHT WAY

We have already discussed in previous chapters the different types of tools, toys, and games that young girls can begin playing with as early as preschool. Some tech-savvy parents and educators may feel like they already actively engage with kids in STEM-themed play, and that is great! But it is important to think about offering girls opportunities to play "the right way" with these tools so that they are building the confidence and skills they need. Consider these actions:

- *Let them figure it out.* Whether animating a story or writing code, whenever possible, allow girls to struggle and figure things out themselves. Offer hints and suggestions when needed, but allowing girls to problem-solve on their own will ultimately build their confidence more in the end. There is no need for anyone to be in tears—but consider giving helpful prompts rather than answers. If you need to demonstrate how to do something, make sure you give kids a chance to try it for themselves afterward.

- *Let them build it themselves.* When building with blocks, LEGOs, crafts, or other materials, adults have a tendency to take over and do it "right" for our children. This is especially true when building by following blueprints or instructions. It is important for adults to exercise restraint in these situations; otherwise, you are taking the learning right out of the girls' hands. It is GREAT to model your excitement about playing with these toys. But consider tinkering with your own pile of LEGOs *next* to your child rather than building something *for* them.
- *Document successes—and failures too.* Parents and educators often take pictures or videos of finished products that come out of kids' STEM play and exploration. But in celebration of the growth mindset, adults should consider taking pictures of the process too, including any struggles or imperfect prototypes along the way.

PROVIDE DIVERSE STEM ROLE MODELS

Parents and educators need to be aware of what young children are seeing on an everyday basis in school, at home, in the media, and in books. Do they see engineers and scientists who look like them? Do they see women and minorities excelling at mathematics and using technology? We have seen in previous chapters how important role-modeling is in children's developing self-concept. It is important for girls to see scientists and engineers who look like them if they will imagine themselves in STEM careers when they grow up.

Try introducing young children to both fictional characters and real-life role models from STEM fields that represent a range of genders, backgrounds, and experiences. Don't know where to start? There are a variety of picture books that showcase fictional girls grappling with STEM concepts, such as *Rosie Revere Engineer* or *Ada Twist Scientist*, both written by Andrea Beaty. For a look at real-world women in STEM, books like *Girls Think of Everything: Stories of Ingenious In-*

ventions by Catherine Thimmesh, and *Women in Science: 50 Fearless Pioneers Who Changed the World* by Rachel Ignotofsky, can help you begin a conversation or choose a historical woman as a focus.

If possible, teachers should also seek out real-world female scientists and engineers to visit the classroom and speak to students. Reach out to children's families for volunteers, and you may be surprised to find connections within your own classroom network. You can also arrange field trips to science museums, makerspaces, and laboratories for an exciting chance to meet female scientists and engineers at work. Local colleges and universities can be a wonderful resource for finding female role models who are majoring in STEM fields and may be interested in coming to your classroom for a visit. Research groups and professors may also be able to help host a field trip to the college campus to see exciting products being developed or engineering students at work!

CHOOSE TOOLS AND ACTIVITIES TO ENGAGE GIRLS

Chapters 9 and 10 introduced a variety of curriculum, technologies, kits, and tools that can be used to engage girls with STEM content beginning in early childhood. There is no shortage of tools and materials available! This wide range of choices can often be difficult for parents and educators. How do you choose the right thing? When deciding on which activity or tool to choose, it is important to do so carefully and come up with topics and themes that will engage the girl(s) with whom you are working. This can be more challenging than it seems, because of course, not all girls like the same thing! Table 11.1 provides some ideas for choosing activities that draw on the interests of your daughters and female students.

There are also a series of questions you can ask yourself when deciding what to try. For example, when choosing gadgets, apps, and technologies, consider the following questions:

- *Does this tool engage girls as creators rather than consumers of digital content?* For girls to succeed in engineering and computer science, they must be creators of digital content, not just consumers of it. Try introducing girls to apps that can teach them to code, software that lets them edit their own movies and photos,

Table 11.1. Ideas for Teaching STEM Based on Girls' Interests

For the Girl Who . . .	STEM Activity Ideas
Loves books and stories	Code alternate endings to your favorite stories using a coding app for young children, such as ScratchJr
Loves the outdoors	Take a nature walk through the woods and learn about plants, animals, and the weather
Loves playing with her friends	Have a STEM-themed sleepover complete with board games like Robot Turtles
Loves cooking	Explore math and measurement in the kitchen through following recipes to bake your favorite dessert
Loves her dolls	Build your own dollhouse using a kit like Roominate
Loves animals	Design, build, and program a robotic pet using a kit like KIBO

kits that allow them to build a robot, or programs that allow them to animate cartoons and stories of their own creation.

- *Will this tool hold girls' attention?* Consider the girl or girls you are purchasing this tool for, and think about whether this will be fun and engaging for five minutes or through multiple uses. Tools that have high "replayability" are sufficiently challenging to keep girls interested, have many levels (or are open-ended) to encourage numerous play sessions, and allow for many different types of discoveries.
- *Is this tool developmentally appropriate?* When focusing on young children, it is important to select tools that are developmentally appropriate, both physically and cognitively. Physically, can the child hold, manipulate, build, and/or navigate this tool with very little adult help? If materials are too challenging or delicate for young children to use on their own, they may lose confidence or interest quickly. Cognitively, are the concepts presented within the child's capacity for understanding? Are concepts presented in an easy-to-understand way? Is there the right amount of text and reading for the age of the child you are considering?
- *Will this tool foster hands-on learning?* The best way for children to learn is by *doing*, not *watching*. Young children especially need opportunities to build and construct with their hands, to practice fine motor skills, and to explore cause and effect through their

own actions. Try to choose tools and technologies that foster hands-on explorations, such as the KIBO robotics kit.

When designing STEM curriculum and activities for girls, ask yourself:

- *Did I choose topics and themes that will engage girls?* Think about the girl or girls you are hoping will participate in this activity. What are their hobbies? What books or shows are they interested in? Science, engineering, and math topics can be integrated across a range of subjects and disciplines. For example, for the girl who is obsessed with fairy tales, try an activity that explores fairy tale engineering. What can you build to help Rapunzel escape the tower? How can we build sturdy houses for the three little pigs that will withstand the wolf's huffing and puffing (i.e., a fan)?
- *Do the tasks allow for collaborative experiences?* While many STEM clubs or programs focus on competition (which usually engages boys more than girls), consider designing collaborative experiences as well. Girls may be more interested in projects if they know they can work with friends. Additionally, they may be more likely to persist through challenges when working collaboratively rather than independently.

FOSTER AWARENESS AND COMPASSION IN BOYS

This book is focused on girls and women. But we need to consider where young boys and men fit into this equation. They are, after all, half the population! In most classrooms and homes, there will be both young boys and girls who need to be engaged with STEM content. For the most part, all of the technologies, teaching tips, and learning advice provided in this chapter are appropriate for children of any gender. Many of the ideas in this book are great ways to engage boys and girls in hands-on projects together! Remember, it is important not only for girls to see themselves succeed in STEM, but for boys to see this as well. Children should see that *everyone* can enjoy making STEM discoveries through hard work and collaboration.

When it comes to reading books about female engineers and scientists, and meeting female role models engaged in STEM, be sure you are not leaving boys out. This is just as important for them to see. All children should grow up seeing diverse role models from a range of backgrounds and genders in order to prevent stereotypes from developing later on. Remember, it is important to talk to boys about the issues presented in this book. Change cannot happen if only half the population is on board. Teachers, parents, and caregivers need to be cognizant of raising compassionate boys who are supportive of others and believe in gender equality in STEM and in all fields. These boys will grow up to be compassionate men who work alongside women to make the needed changes in our society.

TAKE A LOOK AT YOUR OWN BEHAVIOR

Last, but certainly not least, remember to reflect on your own behaviors, biases, and words. Your actions will speak much louder than your words as far as kids are concerned. Sometimes adults unintentionally expect and encourage certain behaviors and traits based on a child's gender. Adults may be more apt to comment on how "cute" or "adorable" girls are and how "tough" or "smart" boys are. Remembering the tips for praising that are rooted in the growth mindset can help stop adults from accidentally using these stereotyped comments.

Adults may also be unknowingly reacting to children's behaviors differently depending on the child's gender. For example, research has shown that when children act assertively, girls tend to be labeled as "bossy," while boys are more likely to be praised for being "leaders" (Martin & Halverson, 1981; Martin & Ruble, 2004; Theimer, Killen, & Stangor, 2001). One way adults can avoid this trap of unintentional gender stereotyping is to *describe* behavior rather than *labeling* or assigning value to behaviors. You can *describe* behavior by saying, "I see you are showing Mark and Sarah how to move these game pieces" rather than *label* the behavior by saying, "You are bossing Mark and Sarah around" or "You are taking the lead on this game."

It is important for adults to be aware of their behaviors and words even when not directly speaking to or interacting with children. Remember, children are always watching and listening, and they are picking up cues from their adult teachers and caregivers. Take stock of your own practices to become aware of any gender biases you may not have noticed. Does dad build all the IKEA furniture? Maybe mom and dad can be cognizant of dividing up this task, or better yet, working *together* the next time something needs to be assembled. Is mom the one who soothes the kids whenever they are scared? Let dad step into the nurturing role next time the kids need it. While it is normal to want to stay in your comfort zone and routine with household and child-rearing tasks, be aware of changing this up every once in a while so that your children do not associate your gender with your skills and abilities.

In the classroom, teachers (all teachers, but especially female teachers) should be aware of modeling their own sense of scientific inquiry. Let kids know when you have a hypothesis you're testing, how you solved an engineering problem, or when math helped you solve a problem in your everyday life. For example, if you are teaching about measurement, you can tell your students about how you used measuring when decorating the classroom walls so that you could pick posters that would fit. Or, if the classroom clock is broken, you can share that you have a hypothesis that the batteries need to be replaced. Be sure to model problem-solving strategies when you don't know the answer to a question a child asks, rather than shying away from it. In this way, you are modeling your own belief in the growth mindset and your abilities to use the STEM skills you are teaching.

Most importantly, model a joy for learning STEM. Show that you enjoy learning about new things, like coding, alongside your students—even if the skill is brand new to you. It is important to demonstrate that anyone can enjoy using STEM skills and approaches with confidence in their everyday lives, whether or not they grow up to be mathematicians and engineers.

REFERENCES

Dweck, C. (2002). Messages that motivate: How praise molds students' beliefs, motivation, and performance (in surprising ways). In J. Aronson (Ed.), *Improving academic achievement: Impact of psychological factors on education* (pp. 37–60). San Diego, CA: Academic Press.

Dweck, C. (2008). *Mindsets and math/science achievement*. New York: Carnegie Foundation, Institute for Advanced Study.

Dweck, C. S., Goetz, T. E., & Strauss, N. L. (1980). Sex differences in learned helplessness: IV. An experimental and naturalistic study of failure generalization and its mediators. *Journal of Personality and Social Psychology, 38*(3), 441.

Johns, M., Schmader, T., & Martens, A. (2005). Knowing is half the battle: Teaching stereotype threat as a means of improving women's math performance. *Psychological Science, 16*(3), 175–179.

Martin, C. L., & Halverson, C. F., Jr. (1981). A schematic processing model of sex typing and stereotyping in children. *Child Development, 52*(4), 1119–1134.

Martin, C. L., & Ruble, D. (2004). Children's search for gender cues: Cognitive perspectives on gender development. *Current Directions in Psychological Science, 13*(2), 67–70.

Theimer, C., Killen, M., & Stangor, C. (2001). Young children's evaluations of exclusion in gender-stereotypic peer contexts. *Developmental Psychology, 37*(1), 18–27.

12

BEYOND EARLY CHILDHOOD

Kristy has always loved coding and robotics. When she was in first grade, her parents got her a Bee-Bot for her birthday, and she loved programming the robot to drive all around her house. At school, she learned to program animations on her iPad using the ScratchJr programming language. Each year, she would program animated greeting cards during the holidays that her parents proudly sent out to their friends and family.

Throughout elementary school, Kristy's parents supported her interest in robotics and coding by signing her up for different robotics summer camps and a Saturday STEAM club. There she was able to socialize with other children who also enjoyed building, tinkering, and coding. By the time Kristy completed elementary school, she confidently uses many different robotics kits, including Bee-Bot, KIBO, and LEGO WeDo. She is also confident when using both ScratchJr and the more complicated Scratch.

When Kristy starts middle school, she sees there is a Scratch Coding Club run in the library after school. She is excited to sign up! She shows up for the first meeting and realizes she is the only girl in the club. Still, she remains in the program because she loves to use Scratch. Eventually, she loses interest in the club when she doesn't make friends and doesn't find people to collaborate on the types of coding projects she likes to work on. Her parents ask her why she left the coding club, and she just shrugs and says she doesn't like it. She tries out a few different STEM clubs throughout middle school, but has slowly lost confidence in her abilities. She makes a lot of new female friends and decides to try out some of the sports and clubs they belong to instead.

In high school, Kristy decides against any Advanced Placement math, science, or computer science classes. Her parents try to encourage her to take them so she has more options later on, but she pleads with them that she does not enjoy these subjects any more. She says they are hard, and that she is not a "math person." Ultimately, Kristy's parents just want her to be happy, and they do not press the subject further, though it saddens them that their daughter has given up on something that once gave her such pride and joy.

LEAKS IN THE PIPELINE

Early childhood has been our focus up to this point . . . and it would be nice if focusing on early interventions was enough to solve the problem of women's underrepresentation in STEM fields. Alas, the gender inequity problem is much more complicated and cannot be solved by placing a band-aid in just one place. Girls and women experience challenges in these fields throughout their education and careers. As we saw in the vignette about Kristy, even girls who love coding or math in early elementary school still need support as they progress through middle school, high school, and beyond in order to keep their interest and confidence in STEM.

Researchers and policymakers often refer to the "STEM pipeline" as a metaphor to demonstrate a student's trajectory through school and into professional STEM career fields. This metaphor is used to illustrate places where there are "leaks" and students "drip out" of the pipeline. In recent years, one focus of the pipeline metaphor has been to demonstrate the proportion of women who "leak out" compared to their male counterparts at various points in the pipeline.

Supporting girls in their early childhood years is an important step that must be taken to address the leaky pipeline situation and set girls up for success. But girls and women need support *throughout* their journeys in order to truly address the gender inequity present in many STEM fields. While it is beyond the scope of this book to deeply delve beyond the early childhood years, this chapter briefly highlights the importance of reaching girls and women at key stages in their development after early childhood.

THE TEENAGE YEARS

The adolescent years are an important time for engaging girls in STEM subjects. This is a time in when gender differences in STEM often become starker. During adolescence, decisions that teenagers make regarding which AP classes to take and which extracurricular clubs to join may have a direct impact on what fields they want to pursue (or will be qualified to pursue) in college.

Teenagers are also in a critical time of identity development and exploration. They are involved in the process of developing identities that will reflect their new social roles as young adults (Eckert, 2000). Teens are also "trying on" different identities during this period in what psychologist Erik Erikson (1963) refers to as a "psychosocial moratorium" relatively free from consequences. This can be an opportunity for teens to "try on" the identity of engineer, creator, or scientist.

Most children enjoy learning STEM concepts at an early age; however, many lose interest by high school (Aschbacher, Li, & Roth, 2010). During their teenage years, many students begin to see math and science as irrelevant to their personal goals (Aschbacher, Li, & Roth, 2010). Prior work has demonstrated that adolescents with talent and interest in mathematics and science are more likely to pursue STEM subjects in postsecondary environments as long as they are also provided with challenging curricula, expert instruction, and peer stimulation (Bloom, 1985; Subotnik, Duschl, & Selmon, 1993; Tai, Liu, Maltese, & Fan, 2006). This demonstrates how important the teenage years are, not only for engaging girls in STEM but increasing girls' *confidence* and *desire* to continue pursuing STEM should they want to.

Adolescence is a wide span of development, by some definitions spanning ages 12–19. During early adolescence (around ages 12–14), girls transition from elementary school into middle school, where they are able to take more control over their classes and extracurricular activities. Prior work has shown that in middle school, girls begin to lose interest in science and mathematics. These early adolescent years are an important time to reach girls because it is during these middle school years that the gender gap begins to emerge in terms of standardized STEM test scores and STEM course taking (Hill, Corbett, & St. Rose, 2010; Spielhagen, 2008). If girls lose interest in STEM during this time, it is less likely that they will be prepared for (or interested in) continuing their STEM education in high school.

During later adolescence (around ages 14–), when they are in high school, young women are in a critical phase of preparing for college and careers. A great deal of the prior research on the STEM pipeline focuses on the aspirations and achievement of high school students (Burkam & Lee, 2003; Madigan, 1997; Maltese & Tai, 2011). This is because the high school years are an important time to gain the preparation and expertise required to pursue many STEM majors in college.

Statistics indicate that one reason men outnumber women in computer science and related majors in college is because female high school students are less likely to take Advanced Placement (AP) exams that could help prepare them to enter these majors (Hill, Corbett, & St. Rose, 2010). In high school, girls are less likely than boys to take numerous college preparatory science and math AP exams, including calculus, computer science, and statistics (Hill, Corbett, & St. Rose, 2010). In order to give young women the option to pursue many STEM fields in college, they must be prepared and encouraged to take these AP exams while they are in high school.

Teenage girls need mentorship, support, and encouragement to pursue these subjects in high school. Educators and parents should show teenage girls (through actions and words) that they believe they can succeed in these courses. They should explain the long-term benefits of exploring these courses and exams, whether or not they go on to become scientists and engineers. High school should be a time for blossoming opportunities, not closing doors.

THE COLLEGE YEARS

Although women make up the majority of college students, they are far less likely than their male peers to plan to major in a STEM field (Hill, Corbett, & St. Rose, 2010). Women have earned more than half (57%) of all bachelor's degrees and about half of all science and engineering bachelor's degrees since the late 1990s. However, women's level of participation in science and engineering fields varies (National Science Foundation, 2017).

In 2009, only 11% of undergraduate computer science degrees from major research universities were granted to women. Over the course of the past decade, the number and proportion of computer sciences bachelor's degrees earned by women has declined (National Science Foundation, 2017). Women's participation in science and engineering fields is highest in psychology, where women account for 70% or more of the graduates at each degree level, while the proportion of women is lowest in engineering, computer sciences, and physics (National Science Foundation, 2017).

It is important to find ways to support women pursuing STEM majors in college and to foster their sense of self-efficacy in these fields. *Self-efficacy* (or one's expectancy of success) is critical in educational and occupational choices (Correll, 2004). Gender differences in interest in STEM can impact technical knowledge and aptitude, creating an ongoing cycle where the lack of knowledge leads to lower self-efficacy and less interest (Schmidt, 2011).

Numerous studies have found that women's computer self-efficacy is lower than men's (Beyer, 2014; Cassidy & Eachus, 2002; Colbeck, Cabrera, & Terenzini, 2001; Salminen-Karlsson, 2009; Zarrett, Malanchuk, Davis-Kean, & Eccles, 2006). Self-confidence and perceived competence in a college student's chosen major can play a role in his or her persistence of the major. For example, Cech et al. (2011) found that in a sample of engineering students from four institutions, self-assessment of one's "professional role competence" is associated with persistence in the engineering major and contributes to the gender gap in college engineering majors.

In the American Association of University Women 's report *Solving the Equation: The Variables for Women's Success in Engineering and Computing*, the authors describe Harvey Mudd College as an example of how changing structures and social environments can result in a dramatic increase in women's representation in computing at the university level (Corbett & Hill, 2015). In five years, the percentage of female Harvey Mudd computer science graduates grew from the historical average of 12% to around 40%, while the national average remains at just 18% (Corbett & Hill, 2015). Now, around 40–50% of computer science majors at Harvey Mudd are women (Sydell, 2017).

According to the AAUW report, Harvey Mudd accomplished this feat through three major changes to the computing environment: revising the introductory computing course and splitting it into two levels divided by experience, providing research opportunities for undergraduates after their first year in college, and taking female students to the Grace Hopper Celebration of Women in Computing conference (Corbett & Hill, 2015). The goal of splitting the introductory course into two levels was to provide a second introductory course for students who had no previous experience in order to reduce the intimidation of enrolling in a class when you have had no prior experience (Sydell, 2017). Finally, Maria Klawe, president of Harvey Mudd College and a computer scientist herself, explained that it was also important to counter negative stereotypes about the computer scientist persona by making it collaborative and involving teamwork rather than making the work lonely or isolating (Sydell, 2017).

It is important for colleges and universities to consider making changes to the environments of their STEM courses and majors. As seen at Harvey Mudd, simple changes can make a world of difference when providing women with opportunities to succeed in these fields. These changes to the social structures may help reach a variety of students who normally would not have been drawn to STEM.

THE CAREER YEARS

Once women have completed STEM majors in college and taken positions in STEM-focused jobs, the battle does not end. Once they have reached this point in the STEM pipeline, women still often "drip out" at higher rates than men. Some research has shown that women in science and engineering exhibit markedly lower retention in their fields over time compared to women in other professional fields (Hunt, 2016; Preston, 2004). For example, prior work has demonstrated that women in STEM fields not only leave the workforce at a higher rate compared to their male counterparts, but they also leave for jobs in other fields at higher rates than men (Preston, 2004).

Why do women leave STEM careers? There are various explanations. Fouad and Singh's (2011) study of women engineers found that nearly half the women in their sample of women with engineering degrees said they left engineering because of lack of advancement or low salary, along with other working conditions. Women in STEM also frequently experience a less positive and supportive work climate in their jobs (Gunter and Stambach, 2005). Compared to women in non-STEM fields, women who work in STEM are more likely to say they have experienced discrimination in the workplace (50% versus 41%) (Funk & Parker, 2018). Very recently, high-profile sexual harassment and gender discrimination complaints and lawsuits against Uber, Twitter, tech venture capitalist firm Kleiner Perkins, and more have brought national attention to an ongoing problem in the workplace environment for women in the technical STEM fields (Benner, 2017).

According to the *New York Times*, the technology industry has suffered from a gender imbalance for some time, with tech giants like Google and Facebook acknowledging that they have very few women in their ranks (Benner, 2017). Current and former employees of Google have spoken in interviews about the ways in which they believe minorities, particularly women of color, are denied equal opportunities and equal pay (Levin, 2017). These employees describe a culture that tolerates racism and sexism (Levin, 2017). In order to increase the retention of women in technical STEM fields, and support fair and safe workplace environments for all people, it is crucial to investigate and address these issues of workplace harassment and discrimination.

WHAT NEEDS TO HAPPEN

It is far past time that those in STEM industries address the issues of sexism, harassment, and inequality that women face in these fields. Research shows that the women who leave STEM fields like engineering are very similar to women who stay in these fields. Instead, it is the *environment* and *workplace culture* that leads to women leaving their STEM jobs. Employers must make it clear that discrimination and harassment of any kind is not tolerated in their workplaces. They must ensure that everyone feels safe and fairly treated in their roles. This includes salary equity as well as opportunities for promotion.

There are other things that employers can do to support women in STEM. For example, improving women's access to mentoring and networks may help support women in STEM (Hunt, 2016). Research has also shown that organizations in which women were less likely to leave also provide clear paths for advancement, gave employees challenging assignments that helped develop and strengthen new skills, and valued and recognized employees' contributions (Corbett & Hill, 2015). To summarize, in order to keep people happy and thriving, employers should focus on providing equitable, safe, and suitably challenging places of business, not just for women, but for all employees.

REFERENCES

Aschbacher, P. R., Li, E., & Roth, E. J. (2010). Is science me? High school students' identities, participation and aspirations in science, engineering, and medicine. *Journal of Research in Science Teaching, 47*(5), 564–582.

Benner, K. (2017, June 30). Women in tech speak frankly on culture of harassment. *New York Times*. Retrieved from https://www.nytimes.com/2017/06/30/technology/women-entrepreneurs-speak-out-sexual-harassment.html

Beyer, S. (2014). Why are women underrepresented in computer science? Gender differences in stereotypes, self-efficacy, values, and interests and predictors of future CS course-taking and grades. *Computer Science Education, 24*(2–3), 153–192.

Bloom, B. S. (Ed.). (1985). *Developing talent in young people*. New York: Ballantine Books.

Burkam, D. T., & Lee, V. E. (2003). *Mathematics, foreign language, and science coursetaking and the NELS:88 transcript data* (NCES 2003-01). Washington, DC: U.S. Department of Education, National Center for Education Statistics.

Cassidy, S., & Eachus, P. (2002). Developing the computer user self-efficacy (CUSE) scale: Investigating the relationship between computer self-efficacy, gender and experience with computers. *Journal of Educational Computing Research, 26*, 133–153.

Cech, E., Rubineau, B., Silbey, S., & Seron, C. (2011). Professional role confidence and gendered persistence in engineering. *American Sociological Review, 76*(5), 641–666.

Colbeck, C. L., Cabrera, A. F., & Terenzini, P. T. (2001). Learning professional confidence: Linking teaching practices, students' self-perceptions, and gender. *Review of Higher Education, 24*, 173–191.

Corbett, C., & Hill, C. (2015). *Solving the equation: The variables for women's success in engineering and computing*. Washington, DC: American Association of University Women.

Correll, S. J. (2004). Constraints into preferences: Gender, status, and emerging career aspirations. *American Sociological Review, 69*, 93–113.

Eckert, P. (2002) Demystifying sexuality and desire. In K. Campbell-Kibler, R. J. Podesva, S. J. Roberts, & A. Wong (Eds.), *Language and sexuality: Contesting meaning in theory and practice* (pp. 99–110). Stanford, CA: CSLI Publications.

Erikson, E. H. (1963). *Childhood and society* (2nd ed.). New York: W. W. Norton.

Fouad, N., & Singh, R. (2011). *Stemming the tide: Why women leave engineering*. Milwaukee, WI: Center for the Study of the Workplace report, University of Wisconsin–Milwaukee.

Funk, C., & Parker, K. (2018). Women and men in STEM often at odds over workplace equity. *Pew Research Centre*.

Gunter, R., & Stambach, A. (2005). Differences in men and women scientists' perceptions of workplace climate. *Journal of Women and Minorities in Science and Engineering, 11*(1), 97–116.

Hill, C., Corbett, C., & St. Rose, A. (2010). *Why so few? Women in science, technology, engineering, and mathematics.* Washington, DC: American Association of University Women.

Hunt, J. (2016). Why do women leave science and engineering? *ILR Review* 69(1), 199–226.

Levin, S. (2017, August 18). Women say they quit Google because of racial discrimination: "I was invisible." *Guardian.* Retrieved from https://www.theguardian.com/technology/2017/aug/18/women-google-memo-racism-sexism-discrimination-quit

Madigan, T. (1997). *Science proficiency and coursetaking in high school: The relationship of science coursetaking patterns to increases in science proficiency between 8th and 12th grades* (NCES 97-838). Washington, DC: U.S. Department of Education, National Center for Education Statistics.

Maltese, A. V., & Tai, R. H. (2011). Pipeline persistence: Examining the association of educational experiences with earned degrees in STEM among US students. *Science Education, 95*(5), 877–907.

National Science Foundation. (2017). *Women, minorities, and persons with disabilities in science and engineering: 2017.* Special Report NSF 17-310. Arlington, VA: National Center for Science and Engineering Statistics. Retrieved from https://www.nsf.gov/statistics/2017/nsf17310/

Preston, A. (2004). *Leaving science: Occupational exit from science careers.* New York: Russell Sage Foundation.

Salminen-Karlsson, M. (2009). Women who learn computing like men: Different gender positions on basic computer courses in adult education. *Journal of Vocational Education and Training, 61*(2), 151–168.

Schmidt, F. (2011). A theory of sex differences in technical aptitude and some supporting evidence. *Perspectives on Psychological Science, 6,* 560–573.

Spielhagen, F. R. (2008). Having it our way: students speak out on single-sex classes. In F. R. Spielhagen (Ed.), *Debating single-sex education: Separate and equal* (pp. 32–46). Lanham, MD: Rowman & Littlefield.

Subotnik, R. F., Duschl, R., & Selmon, E. (1993). Retention and attrition of science talent: A longitudinal study of Westinghouse Science Talent Search winners. *International Journal of Science Education, 15*(6), 1–72.

Sydell, L. (2017). Colleges have increased computer science majors: What can Google learn? *National Public Radio: All Tech Considered.* Retrieved from https://www.npr.org/sections/alltechconsidered/2017/08/10/542638758/colleges-have-increased-women-computer-science-majors-what-can-google-learn

Tai, R. H., Liu, C. Q., Maltese, A. V., & Fan, X. (2006). Planning early for careers in science. *Science, 312,* 1143–1144.

Zarrett, N. R., Malanchuk, O., Davis-Kean, P. E., & Eccles, J. (2006). Examining the gender gap in IT by race: Young adults' decisions to pursue an IT career. In J. M. Cohoon & W. Aspray (Eds.), *Women and information technology* (pp. 55–88). Cambridge, MA: MIT Press.

CONCLUSION

Imagining the Scientists and Engineers of the Future

The products of scientific and technological innovation, from cell phones to pharmaceuticals, help to ease and enrich our lives in significant ways. But when women are left out of the process, science suffers, and we suffer.

—Linda Hallman, executive director, American Association of University Women (AAUW)

Diversity of all kinds is critical to the success of our country's STEM industry. Drawing on the unique experiences and opinions of people from different backgrounds sparks the right debates and conversations that lead to the most powerful kinds of innovation. When women are removed from this process, science and technical fields cannot move forward and evolve the way they should. Without women, progress is stunted—it is as simple as that. For this reason, the underrepresentation of women in STEM fields has been a growing cause of concern to researchers, feminists, and policymakers for the last five decades.

With research findings on women in STEM being widely disseminated to the general public in recent years, this gender divide is now becoming a growing concern outside the academic sphere. Now, we see that parents, teachers, and caregivers are becoming increasingly invested in addressing this divide. These individuals—many of whom are the readers of this book—have the power to make real and lasting change regarding this gender disparity.

Most educators, parents, and caregivers already know that early childhood is an important and beautiful time in human development. They see young children rapidly gaining physical skills and reaching impressive cognitive milestones. These early experiences are so significant in the long-term development of children. Something as simple as the types of play we encourage children to engage in or the types of toys we provide can have lasting impacts.

Research has shown that building and tinkering during one's childhood serves as beneficial in an engineering career later in life, and that women often have little experience with childhood tinkering compared to men. In order to support future generations of scientists, engineers, and inventors, it is important to provide children of all genders with toys and technologies that let them build, create, problem-solve, and tinker.

STEREOTYPES AND BIASES REVISITED

Sexism and gender stereotyping can take many shapes and forms. They can take the form of passing comments or microaggressions. They can take the form of overt harassment. They can take the form of discrimination or insults. They can take the form of discouragement. Sexism and gender stereotyping can happen so seamlessly and in such subtle ways that you do not even realize you are on the receiving end of sexism—or that *you* are the one perpetuating the bias.

We all have stereotypes. We all have biases. Sometimes, we have biases that we stop ourselves from acting on. Sometimes we don't even realize the biases we have. It is important to stop and think about our implicit biases and the automatic reactions that we have. Most of us want to think that we don't have any biases. In this case, ignorance is *not* bliss. Actions and behaviors can only change once we are aware of them. There are some wonderful online resources that deal with learning about our own implicit biases in order to prompt us to take a hard look at our own beliefs.

One of the most famous resources is Project Implicit, (https:// implicit.harvard.edu/implicit/), a nonprofit organization and collaboration among researchers who are interested in implicit thinking (i.e., thoughts, feelings, and reactions outside of our conscious awareness and control). The goal of Project Implicit is to inform the public about the "hidden biases" that influence us.

Project Implicit offers many different online tests you can take that pertain to implicit attitudes regarding race, gender, religion, and more. Two tests of particular relevance to STEM gender stereotypes are the Gender-Science test and Gender-Career test (you can take these tests at https://implicit.harvard.edu/implicit/selectatest.html). Taking tests like these are often great conversation starters with colleagues, family, and friends about the widespread nature of biases. Honest self-reflection and communication can be the first step in making changes and stopping the perpetuation of gender stereotypes.

Adults often do not realize the degree to which young children are watching them, observing them, and picking up on the things that they say and do. If adults want to dispel gender stereotypes in the young children they work and live with, it is critical that they first take stock of their own behaviors and biases.

IMAGINING FUTURE SCIENTISTS AND ENGINEERS

When you began reading this book, you were asked to picture the person who made the computer, tablet, or e-reader on which you are reading it, or the website from which you have purchased it. You stopped to think about what their personality traits might be or what their jobs might be like. It is likely that, whether you believe them or not, some stereotypes came to mind about a person working in the technology industry. It is important to reach young children early, before they have ingrained these same cultural stereotypes. It is important for them to see STEM as fun, creative, and social endeavors. That STEM can be masculine or feminine or neither. STEM can be about solving problems, inventing new things, or making things easier and helping people. It can be just as much about creating beautiful things as it is about creating powerful things. There are so many different kinds of STEM careers out there (see appendix B for some ideas to talk to children about).

In chapter 9, we explored the idea of "designing beyond the default." If the default image of STEM is that it is hard and complicated work, or that it is all about working on battling robots or sitting alone to write lines of code, then we will only ever reach the same kinds of kids and adults. It is time to counter these stereotypes by providing girls—and all children—with new kinds of STEM apps, games, toys, and tools that will open their minds to the social, fun, collaborative, and creative things that can be done in STEM fields. Whether or not they grow up to be scientists or engineers, all young children should be able see these fields as possibilities, and have equal opportunities to pursue them if they decide to.

WISHES FOR THE NEXT GENERATION

To the next generation of teachers, engineers, scientists, inventors, artists, writers, and designers who are just young children at the time this book is being written: Remember that you can achieve great things through persistence and hard work. Remember that you are not defined by your gender identity, your sex, your race, your physical appearance, or any other attribute that labels you. Do not allow society's expectations to shape your journey. Dream big. Then work hard to achieve those dreams. Your possibilities are endless.

APPENDIX A
Gender Divide in STEM Factsheet

Fact: Men continue to outnumber women in many STEM fields such as engineering and computer science.

- Women currently make up less than 15% of engineers and only 26% of computer scientists and mathematicians.

Fact: We need more technical professionals. In the next decade, it is estimated that the United States will need 1.7 million more engineers and computing profession.

- Increasing the interest of women in these fields will help to fill these roles.
- The views and experiences of women must be considered when making scientific and technological advancements.

Fact: Girls' and women's performance in STEM fields may be negatively impacted by a phenomenon known as "stereotype threat."

- Stereotype threat is the anxiety produced by the feeling that one's performance will be seen through the lens of a negative stereotype.

Fact: Girls and women need to be supported in STEM, beginning in early childhood.

- Girls often have less experience with tinkering and building in early childhood. It is important to provide girls with opportunities to build, code, and explore all aspects of STEM, beginning in pre-kindergarten.

APPENDIX B
STEM Career Examples

Adults should begin talking to young children about the many different types of STEM-related careers available. Here is a short list of career examples to get you started.

STEM Area	Career Examples
Science	doctor, marine biologist, chemist, zoologist
Technology	computer programmer, website designer, videogame developer, app developer
Engineering	environmental engineer, biomedical engineer, aerospace engineer
Mathematics	statistician, mathematics professor, data scientist

APPENDIX C

Planning Sheet for Educators: Designing STEAM Curriculum to Engage Girls

Use the prompts below to brainstorm the curriculum or activity you are planning to implement. Think about your answers to these questions to help create a well-rounded plan.

- **TOPIC:** What STEAM topic(s) will you explore?
- **TIME:** How much time will you have to devote to this topic? Will it be a long curriulum, taking place in small increments over an extended period? Or will it be a one-off exploration?
- **AUDIENCE:** Who will be completing this curriculum/activity? What are their ages and developmental needs? Are you reaching just girls, or children of all genders?
- **PREPARATION:** What will you need to prepare to teach this? Will you need extra training yourself (for example, learning how to use a new technology)?
- **SPECIFIC ACTIVITIES:** What specific activities will you be doing to explore your topic? Why do you think these activities will be appealing to girls?
- **LOGISTICS:** What materials will you need? What are other logistics you need to plan for (such as grouping kids)?

APPENDIX D
STEM Picture Books

The books listed here are a few suggestions wonderful picture books to begin exploring science and engineering with young children during story time at home or school.

STEM BOOKS FEATURING FEMALE CHARACTERS

The Most Magnificent Thing by Ashley Spires (Toronto, ON: Kids Can Press, 2014).

Rosie Revere, Engineer by Andrea Beaty (New York, NY: Abrams Books for Young Readers, 2013).

Ada Twist, Scientist by Andrea Beaty (New York, NY: Abrams Books for Young Readers, 2016).

The Girl Who Thought in Pictures: The Story of Dr. Temple Grandin, by Julia Finley Mosca (Seattle, WA: Innovation Press, 2017).

BOOKS ABOUT BUILDING AND DESIGN

Dreaming Up: A Celebration of Building by Christy Hale (New York, NY: Lee & Low Books, 2012).

If I Built a Car by Chris Van Dusen (New York, NY: Puffin Books, 2005).

If I Built a House by Chris Van Dusen (New York: Dial Books, 2012).

Iggy Peck, Architect by Andrea Beaty (New York, NY: Abrams Books for Young Readers, 2007).

BOOKS ABOUT MATH, SCIENCE, AND MORE

The Boy Who Loved Math: The Improbable Life of Paul Erdos by Deborah Heiligman (New York, NY: Roaring Book Press, 2013).

The Grapes of Math by Greg Tang (New York, NY: Scholastic, 2001).

This Little Scientist by Joan Holub (New York, NY: Little Simon, 2018).

Scientist, Scientist, Who Do You See? by Chris Ferrie (Naperville, IL: Sourcebooks Jabberwocky, 2018).

Quantum Physics for Babies by Chris Ferrie (Naperville, IL: Sourcebooks Jabberwocky, 2013).

ABOUT THE AUTHOR

Amanda Alzena Sullivan, PhD, is a child development specialist who studies the impact of new technologies and media on children. Amanda's research is specifically concerned with using new technologies to engage girls in STEM (science, technology, engineering, and mathematics) in order to increase the representation of girls and women in these fields. Her research on gender and technology has been published in numerous academic research journals and has been featured in popular outlets such as *WIRED* and *EdWeek*.

Amanda received her master and doctoral degrees in child development at the Eliot-Pearson Department of Child Study and Human Development at Tufts University, where she conducted research with the Developmental Technologies (DevTech) Research Group. Amanda contributed to the creation of several educational technology interfaces prototyped at DevTech, and is the cocreator of the ScratchJr Coding Cards published by No Starch Press.

Amanda is also the mother of an energetic little boy, and a longtime educator who loves working with young children. She has over a decade of experience teaching drama, film production, STEM, STEAM, robotics, coding, and more at the early childhood and elementary level.